TWAYNE'S WORLD LEADERS SERIES

EDITOR OF THIS VOLUME

Samuel Smith, Ph.D.

Robert Owen as Educator

TWLS 60

Robert Owen

Robert Owen
As Educator

By KAREN CAPLAN ALTFEST

TWAYNE PUBLISHERS

A DIVISION OF G. K. HALL & CO., BOSTON

Library of Congress Cataloging in Publication Data

Altfest, Karen Caplan.
  Robert Owen as educator.

  (Twayne's world leaders series ; TWLS 60)
  Bibliography: p. 181 - 87.
  Includes index.
  1. Owen, Robert, 1771 - 1858. 2. Teachers—Great
Britain—Biography. I.   Title.
LA2375.G72093   370'.92'4 [B]   77-23512
ISBN 0-8057-7711-3

For Lew

Contents

About the Author

Karen Caplan Altfest, a native of Montreal, Canada, received her M.A. degree in history from Hunter College. Mrs. Altfest, a member of Phi Alpha Theta, is a candidate for a Ph.D. in history at the Graduate School and University Center of The City University of New York and is writing a dissertation on Canadian nationalism.

Preface

In our ever-changing world it is noteworthy that numerous innovations in the field of education recommended by Robert Owen more than a century ago are still much in use today. Owen's educational reforms, often considered excessively visionary in his own lifetime, have gradually won acceptance in various forms throughout the Western world. Historical events have tended more and more to vindicate his views on human nature and society.

Education was central to Owen's career as a great social reformer. This book analyzes his educational ideas, ideals, experiments, and accomplishments in considerable detail, for it was by educating children and reeducating adults that he expected to accomplish the reconstruction of society. He was not merely an innovative educator in a narrow sense but a liberal industrialist, experimental socialist, philanthropist, and dedicated moral philosopher. His multi-faceted character has not been ignored in this book, for all the principal aspects of his personality, career, and influence played a part in enabling him to pioneer in such important areas as infant schools and early childhood education, vocational training, adult education, visual education, methods of teaching, and teacher training. The total man has been portrayed the better to illuminate the role of Owen as educator.

Acknowledgment should be made to Dr. Samuel Smith, editor of educational books in this series, for his information and assistance. I am especially grateful to Frances Minters for valuable suggestions during the preparation of the manuscript. To my parents, Betty and Philip Caplan, I wish to express appreciation for their encouragement, and to my daughter, Ellen Wendy Altfest, for immeasurable patience. And I wish to thank my husband, Lewis J. Altfest, who has been supportive and encouraging in this endeavor as in all aspects of my career.

KAREN CAPLAN ALTFEST

Chronology

1771   Born May 14 at Newtown, North Wales.

1778   Appointed as assistant teacher and school usher.

1781   Left home to work in London clothing shop.

1789   Entered into partnership in Manchester machinery factory.

1790   Accepted position as plant manager of Drinkwater mill.

1794   Became manager and partner in Chorlton Twist Company, Manchester. Gave financial aid to Robert Fulton.

1797   Purchased New Lanark mills from David Dale with partners.

1799   Married to Anne Caroline Dale.

1803   Reported on the state of the cotton trade of Great Britain to the Glasgow Committee of Manufacturers.

1809   Opened first Infant School, New Lanark.

1813   Published "Essays on the Formation of Character" and "A New View of Society."

1816   Opened the New Institution for the Formation of Character.

1818   Toured the Continent, visiting Pestalozzi and Fellenberg.

1819   Replaced headmaster Buchanan, who resigned to manage infant school in Westminster.

1825   Purchased New Harmony, Indiana, with William Maclure as partner. Addressed the Congress of the United States, February 25 and March 7.

1826   "Boatload of Knowledge"—scientists and other scholars—arrived at New Harmony.

1827   Farewell Address, May 27, at New Harmony.

1829   Sold interest in New Lanark.

1831   Wife, Anne Caroline Dale Owen, died.

1832 -   Edited *The Crisis*.
1834

1836   Published *Book of the New Moral World*.

1838 -   Supervised Queenwood Community.
1839

1851 - Edited *Robert Owen's Journal.*
1852
1853   Published *Rational Quarterly Review and Journal.*
1856 - Published *Millenial Gazette.*
1858
1857   Wrote *The Life of Robert Owen.*
1858   Died at Newtown on November 17.

CHAPTER 1

Biographical Introduction

R OBERT Owen was a successful manufacturer, labor leader, philanthropist, social reformer, and experimental educator—a versatile pioneer who believed that he had a mission in life, one central motif, which he delineated as follows in his autobiography:

The mission of my life appears to be, to prepare the population of the world to understand the vast importance of the second creation of humanity, from the birth of each individual, through the agency of man, by creating entirely new surroundings in which to place all through life, and by which a new human nature would appear to arise from new surroundings.

That mission has been to point out to humanity the way to remove from it the cause of sin and misery, and how in place thereof to attain for all of our race in perpetuity a new existence of universal goodness, wisdom, and happiness, and to withdraw from man all unkindness to man and even to animal life over the earth, so far as may be consistent with his own happy progress while upon it.[1]

Owen's life was devoted to convincing the world of the validity of his mission, thus pointing the way to drastic reforms in education and society. Owen felt that he was merely an agent of a greater force, that he deserved no special credit or rewards for his contributions to social progress, that he was destined to be the prophet of a revolutionary change that would inevitably occur.

He considered the credentials for his assignment in life to be a profound understanding of human nature and a clear vision of the new social conditions that would be necessary in order to remake and perfect mankind. He noted that his credentials as a social reformer came from

reading and reflection, from practice, and from personal communication.

To make myself acquainted with the facts to be collected from the past history of our species, I read, in my early life, at least five hours each day, on an average of twenty years . . . .

To ascertain whether the principles which the reading of those facts, and the reflections thereon, produced in my mind, were true, and, if true, beneficial for practice, I commenced a series of experiments, which have now continued, without intermission, for nearly thirty-five years.[2]

Thus he attributed to his readings and early education the grand vision of social and educational reforms which was to contribute significantly to the progress of society. Steadfastly he devoted himself to the task of demonstrating through his writings, discussions, and practical experiments the fact that environmental changes and new social arrangements could nobly transform human nature and achieve utopian ends.

I *Childhood Years*

Many of the ideas and ideals explicitly formulated by Owen in later life can be seen to have germinated during his early childhood. He was born May 14, 1771, at Newtown, Montgomery, in North Wales, a small market town with a population of no more than a thousand. Robert, the second youngest of seven children in his family (two of whom had died in infancy), was intellectually and physically precocious. His father was a saddler, ironmonger, and local postmaster who kept a shop in the front part of his house. Mr. Owen laid down rigid rules of behavior for the children, but he doted on his gifted son, and only once did he impose harsh physical discipline upon him. From the paternal example of love and understanding the boy learned the value of kindness and tolerance contrasted with the customary resort to corporal punishment of children, a form of discipline which Owen rejected and condemned throughout his lifetime. His parents showed respect for his intelligence by consulting him regarding important family problems. Mutual respect and good example proved to be much more effective than strict discipline as a means of inculcating desirable character traits.

This relationship was to form the basis of Owen's later theories of child training. He never forgot the beneficent effects of paternal understanding and respect upon his character and he later applied the same principles to the rearing of his own children. He did not punish them for misbehavior but instead explained in which way their actions had caused someone unhappiness. Often he reminded them: "I have never struck you. You must never strike anybody."[3] His wife, however, believed in corporal punishment as an effective method of discipline. He had to persuade her that discussion and explanation are far superior means of expressing parental disapproval and preventing children from becoming "ungovernable."[4] At the same time, he did not praise the children for their good behavior, although he would sometimes express approval by means of a smile or caress and was generally considered to be a sympathetic, indulgent father. Since the children were not accustomed to praise, they were said to have reacted excessively, as if "intoxicated" with joy, when strangers bestowed it upon them. Owen discouraged rivalry for the sake of social approval or rewards, and later recalled that such competition had driven him and his brother apart. He encouraged independent decision-making which, he felt, had given him an early start on the road to adult life.

When he was about four or five years old, Owen was enrolled in a small school administered by a local teacher, Mr. Thickness. There he learned to read efficiently, to write legibly, and to understand the "first four rules of arithmetic."[5] In his autobiography he noted that he had found the school activities to be diversified and enjoyable. Yet he learned only to speak "ungrammatically, a kind of Welsh English . . . which was an imperfect mixture of both languages."[6] When he moved to England he was greatly embarrassed by his accent and was painfully aware of an inability to express his thoughts clearly and forcefully.

Owen did not limit himself to the basic skills of the school curriculum. He also excelled in dancing and track and field sports. He was talented musically, a skilled clarinetist. By age seven he had acquired the essentials of a well-rounded elementary education.

At this time, only seven years old, Owen was appointed by Mr. Thickness to be an assistant teacher and usher in the school, assigned to helping other boys to master the rudiments which he had already learned, and he in this way earned enough to pay his own tuition, relieving his father of that financial burden. His duties took up most of his time but his own education did not suffer, for he had apparently learned all that Mr. Thickness could teach him.

Moreover, the work familiarized him with the learning problems of children and instilled in him a lasting interest in teaching.

In later life Owen recalled that he had been a favorite of the townspeople and perhaps had been too much indulged for his own good. He was an exceptional child. His display of superiority in contests with older children won him applause and popularity. But his serious attitude and habits of deep reflection about many subjects set him apart from children of his own age, a problem augmented by the fact that bad reactions to common foods often kept him from joining them at meals. One of his few friends was a young student of theology by whom he was inspired to enjoy "cultivated taste and superior conversation"[7] and to acquire enduring interest in the laws and beauty of nature.

Robert always found time for his favorite subject, reading, from which he derived utmost satisfaction and inspiration. He read virtually all the worthwhile books available in Newtown, borrowing them from the local clergyman, physician, and attorney, sympathetic and learned men of the community who gladly furthered the education of this earnest, intelligent, and diligent boy. Often Owen recalled how much enjoyment and useful information he had derived from reading classical works, such as *Robinson Crusoe*, *Pilgrim's Progress*, and *Paradise Lost*, as well as travel books, ancient history books, religious works, and biographies of philosophers and other great thinkers. Nevertheless, paradoxically, he eventually opposed the use of literary works in classroom instruction because in his judgment they did not serve the interests and educational needs of most young children.

II   *Business Ventures*

At the age of nine years, realizing that his own formal education had come to a standstill and that nothing more was to be gained from his duties at the school, Owen gave up teaching and was employed for two years as an assistant to a local draper and haberdasher. At the end of that period he decided there was no future in working for a small enterprise of that sort and, furthermore, even though he enjoyed the clean, attractive environment, he disliked many of the manners and customs, the way of life, in a small town. Therefore he determined to seek his fortune elsewhere.

He was only ten years old when he made his way to London, where he became proudly self-supporting. His older brother William, a saddler, obtained a position for him as an assistant to James McGuffog, dealer in women's clothing who owned a shop in Stamford, Lincolnshire. McGuffog, a kindly and competent employer, taught him business procedures and impressed upon him the values of honesty, order, and accuracy as prerequisites of business success. Compensation during the first year, which was considered a training period, consisted only of room and board, customarily provided by employers, supplemented in the second year by a salary of £8 and in the third year by a salary of £10. He was treated not as a mere employee but rather as a member of the McGuffog family and was rarely reproached or criticized. McGuffog made his well-stocked library available to the boy, who continued to read about five hours daily.

Owen made rapid progress in his commercial career. He remained with McGuffog four years, during which time he became a skilled craftsman in handling fine fabrics and learned how to do business with an upper-class clientele. Then, eager to increase his knowledge and experience, he accepted a position as a salesman in a London shop (Flint and Palmer) at a salary of £25 per annum in addition to room and board. When this work became too tedious and burdensome, he began to seek out new opportunities. Soon he accepted another sales position, this one in Manchester, which paid him a higher salary (£40 per annum), but after a while he felt dissatisfied with his role as an employee and resolved to become an independent businessman. Now eighteen years of age, he gave up his new position and borrowed £100 from his brother in order to set up a shop for manufacturing machinery in partnership with an acquaintance named Jones who had had some experience as a manufacturer of wire-bonnet frames.

This venture prospered so well that the partners soon had forty employees. Jones was in charge of manufacturing while Owen handled the accounts and supervised the workers. The relationship between the partners grew strained, however, mainly because Jones was not a good businessman, and within a few months Owen sold his share of the enterprise in exchange for six machines (only three of which he actually received) and some yarn. Declining an offer of partnership from the wealthy McGuffog, Owen, at the age of nineteen, then started his own business, spinning yarn and selling it to manufacturers in Glasgow.

The business was quite prosperous. Nevertheless, Owen, always alert to new opportunities, readily gave it up in order to accept a very well paid position of great responsibility as plant manager for a mill in Manchester owned by a wealthy manufacturer and merchant named Drinkwater. Now, at twenty years of age, he was in charge of five hundred workers. Other manufacturers predicted that disaster would result from the hiring of so young a man for so large a task, but Owen applied himself with such vigor to his new role that it took him only six weeks of application and observation to master the situation. His habits of self-discipline, exactness, and keen perception served him well. He made a careful study of the machinery in the mill and became the first to use such machinery for spinning cotton, producing a higher quality of product and increasing production and profits for the firm.

During the first six months in the business he gained invaluable experience, for his duties included purchasing goods, supervising the manufacture of cotton into yarn, selling the finished products, keeping accounts, and paying wages to employees, and he earned the reputation of being a fair and competent manager. He won the trust of his workers, persuading them to maintain habits of order, discipline, regularity, and sobriety. He was then offered and accepted a one-fourth partnership in the business. Now the same merchants who had predicted failure welcomed Owen's friendship. Being completely absorbed in his business, however, and still feeling awkward about his Welsh accent and his provincial manners, he remained aloof.

Drinkwater owned another cotton mill, in Cheshire. In 1792 Owen performed the difficult task of successfully reorganizing the Cheshire plant while at the same time managing production in Manchester by commuting between the two mills. Shortly thereafter, however, when Drinkwater's daughter married, the son-in-law, who wished to restrict ownership of the business to the family, induced Owen to give up his partnership interest.

Owen had become expert in the problems of cotton-spinning and the textile trade, ranking with such important pioneers as Sir Richard Arkwright and Sir Robert Peel in the organization of the factory system. His competence and contributions were rewarded with material success (when not yet twenty years old he was earning £300 per annum, a large salary in those days), but the accumulation of wealth was not his primary motivation. He had broader interests than financial security or income. Thus it is worth noting that he came to the assistance of Robert Fulton whose experiments in spinning flax and in rope-making as well as navigation and transportation held out promise of improved living conditions for the masses. Owen's broad interests were further reflected in his application for membership in the Literary and Philosophical Society of Manchester.

At meetings of this society Owen was called upon for his opinions on problems of the cotton-spinning trade. At first he felt awkward, ill at ease, at times almost incoherent, unable to make his knowledge available to the audience, yet he persisted in his membership activities until through hard experience and self-discipline he acquired excellent skill in written and oral communication of his views. In Manchester he began to develop the style of oratory for which he became well known in later years.

His eagerness to learn, his ability to apply himself to any task until it had been well done, and his persistent quest for self-improvement were the principal motivating factors in personal affairs as in his business career. He never balked at hard work, never sought immediate gratification at the expense of wider future goals. He was consistent, steadfast, not easily swayed once his mind had been made up. His success in business and all his other notable accomplishments must be attributed in large part to determination, disciplined intelligence, and strength of character, as well as to a natural ability to inspire people with confidence. He has been aptly described as a person exhibiting a "childlike simplicity of character, and at the same time [being] one of the born leaders of men."[8] This seeming inconsistency in Owen's personality served to disarm his opponents and competitors, not impeding but contributing to his further successes.

III *Introduction to New Lanark*

In 1794 Owen again became proprietor of a business, this time at Chorlton in Manchester, where, in association with two well-known firms (Messrs. Borrodale and Atkinson of London, and Messrs. Barton of Manchester) he managed the Chorlton Twist Company. During his superintendence, extending over a period of two or three years, a large factory was built and equipped with excellent, new machines. His principal duties as manager were to purchase cotton, see to it that it was manufactured into yarn of high quality, and sell the yarn. Thomas Atkinson, who assisted him, kept the books. Owen travelled regularly by coach to manufacturing towns in Lancashire as well as to the west of Scotland. These trips widened his circle of acquaintances within the prosperous mercantile and intellectual classes and also enabled him to witness firsthand the contrast between their favorable situation and the wretched living conditions of the working class.

On one of his frequent business journeys to Glasgow he met and fell in love with Anne Caroline Dale, daughter of David Dale, a wealthy, self-made Scottish industrialist "who was then one of the most extraordinary men in the commercial world of Scotland,—an extensive manufacturer, cotton-spinner, merchant, banker, and preacher."[9] Dale, who was "universally trusted and respected,"[10] was the proprietor of cotton-spinning mills located at New Lanark, about thirty miles from Glasgow.

Anne Caroline Dale encouraged his affections but he knew she would not marry him without her father's consent, which, owing to Owen's short acquaintance with the family and to differences in their religious affiliations (Dale was leader of a sect of Independent Presbyterian dissenters from the Church of Scotland)[11] would be very difficult to obtain. (Owen's autobiography explains the situation as follows: "Her father's religious character, his high standing in society, and my not knowing him, would have deterred me from aspiring to such a position as to become his son-in-law.")[12] Therefore Owen decided to approach Dale, not as a suitor for his daughter's hand but as a businessman interested in purchasing the New Lanark mills. (At this time Dale was considering retirement from his business.) Before long Owen won Dale's confidence and, in fact, in 1797, when twenty-seven, he became a proprietor of the mills which he and his partners purchased for £60,000.

In later years Owen recalled that Dale at first opposed any personal involvement between his daughter and the aggressive young man, but eventually "his cold and distant manner to me [Owen] gradually diminished, until he began to be more at ease when we met, and at length he relaxed so far in his manner as to receive me pleasantly, and after a little time in a friendly and almost cordial manner."[13] Owen and Anne Caroline finally wore down Dale's resistance and married in 1799. Determination and perseverance had, as they would often in Owen's future, proved themselves to be the dominating aspects of his character.

Acquisition of the New Lanark mills gave Owen his first opportunity to experiment with new ideas concerning cooperative living and education which he had earlier formulated and had hoped some day to put into practice.

CHAPTER 2

Owen as Social Reformer

G REAT Britain, in the late eighteenth century, was being
transformed rapidly from an agricultural into an industrial
nation. New machines designed to increase the efficiency of
production eliminated many small, family-run farms and cottage industries which were replaced in the economic structure by factories
and mills. The Industrial Revolution, soon to spread from England
to other European countries, was accompanied in its early stages by
drastic social changes, the most important of which were a rapid
growth of population, a shifting of population to the North and
West of England, urbanization, and new or intensified social
problems, such as the spread of disease and malnutrition, slum
housing, and poverty, all reflected in a widening gap between the
very rich and very poor classes of society.

I Technological Developments

The staple industry of eighteenth-century England was the spinning and weaving of woolen goods. But the infant cotton industry
was growing rapidly; it required mechanization. The machines
commonly used prior to the onset of industrialization were the spinning wheel and the handloom, both limited to small-scale production. In mid-century the introduction of new, more efficient
machines, capable of producing goods speedily in much larger
volume, necessitated the reorganization of the manufacturing
system.

John Kay's flying shuttle (1733) permitted a broader width of
material to be woven and attained a much higher speed of operation than had previously been possible. James Hargreaves invented

22

the spinning-jenny (1767) which enabled the worker to spin several threads simultaneously. Richard Arkwright used a water frame for spinning (about 1769) which was run by water power. Samuel Compton developed the spinning mule (1779) which combined features of the spinning-jenny and the water frame and produced thread that was very fine and strong. Edmund Cartwright constructed a power loom (1785) for weaving. Machines were now doing the jobs of men and women much more rapidly, producing goods of higher quality and in greater abundance than ever before. James Watt's improvements (1769) upon Thomas Newcomen's steam engine eventually resulted in the use of steam instead of water as a source of power in many situations; the steamboat and locomotive transformed transportation and navigation. The pioneering inventors of the time were all practical-minded technicians, not concerned with scientific theory but striving to improve methods of production and distribution.

The city of Manchester, which had long prospered owing to its favorable location for navigation and trade, was becoming the industrial center of Great Britain. Its manufacturers had specialized in the production of woolen goods; it had also developed an extensive cotton industry during the seventeenth century, a hundred years before cotton threatened to replace wool as Britain's staple manufacture. The building of two canals leading to the city facilitated transportation. The Duke of Bridgewater built the Worsley Canal in 1761, and its extension became the Mersey Canal, opened in 1822. In keeping with a general growth in population during the Industrial Revolution, according to census records the population of Manchester and Salford increased from 27,000 in 1773 to 84,000 in 1801. As more and more factories were built during the nineteenth century, Manchester retained its status as the foremost industrial center of the nation.

With the advent of steam power the mills and factories, no longer dependent on water power, could be built at sites closer to their raw materials and more accessible to customers. Drinkwater's mill, where Owen worked, was one of the first mills to make use of steam power. The rapid expansion of the coal and iron industries gave further impetus to utilization of the steam engine and speeded the development of large-scale production in Great Britain.

II *Status of the Working Class*

Along with demographic and industrial change, class realignment occurred during this period of industrialization. A new British working class arose, and it developed a certain cohesiveness required in order to give expression to its discontents. The workers, subjected to economic exploitation, political oppression, and social deprivation, protested through such means as trade unions and periodicals and, in some instances, rioted against the machines which seemed to threaten their security.[1] As a higher standard of living became attainable the value system was altered. People focused on material needs and neglected moral ones. The shift in goals, the change in working conditions, and the development of new groups within society necessitated a redefinition of inter-personal and inter-class relationships. As one historian wrote,

The Industrial Revolution was more than the coming of machines driven by steam. It was more than a rapid spread of factories pouring out goods in an ever-increasing volume. It was also a revolution changing the thoughts and practices of men. Laws adapted to an agricultural economy became obsolete. Long established employee-employer relationships based on the small shop ceased to function; the old personal tie gave way to an impersonal one. The new captains of industry, removed from their employees, were little concerned with their comfort and well-being. Regard for profits and more profits occupied their waking thoughts. A newly rich class sprang up; and, after their kind, they behaved in ways unbelievably calloused.[2]

The old ruling class, now being challenged by wealthy industrialists, struggled to retain supremacy in the social order. Although the new class of industrialists did not possess the titles, family connections, or authority traditionally enjoyed by the landed aristocracy, they often had more money than the aristocrats and soon demanded political power commensurate with their financial status.

By the end of the eighteenth century British workers had begun to organize in an attempt to obtain higher wages and better working conditions. Boycotts, petitions, demonstrations, mass meetings, and riots were principal methods used to call attention to their grievances. Reactionary politicians and manufacturers regarded workers' associations as revolutionary organizations and attempted to restrict or destroy them. The parliamentary acts of 1720 and 1744 had prohibited workers' combinations (unions). In 1799 the Workmen's Combination Bill outlawed any association formed to obtain higher wages, shorter hours, or the employment of progressive-minded workers to the exclusion of others. Nevertheless, secret meetings of workers' organizations could not be altogether suppressed, and labor agitation continued.

In Britain at this time, owing largely to the efforts of philanthropists like Robert Owen and particularly to a religious revival (stimulated by John Wesley's Methodist movement stressing the need for brotherhood and improved working conditions), it was generally acknowledged that the well-to-do had a duty to care for the virtuous poor. Notwithstanding the charity dispensed by local churches, however, the established Anglican church continued to cater to the upper classes and property interests. The sad plight of the destitute poor was taken for granted as more and more of them were confined to miserable poorhouses. Factory owners concerned themselves, not with the care of their workers, but only with their productivity. Many of the new capitalists were dissenters from the established church anyway, not troubled very much about moral obligations to their fellow man. The Poor Law authorizing the state to administer charity was designed to reduce begging on the streets and provide minimal aid for the needy, but the remedy proved most often to be as harsh as the disease. To qualify for public assistance, applicants had to proclaim themselves publicly as indigents, move into living quarters unfit for human habitation, and still pay for bare subsistence with hard labor. All but the most hopelessly destitute or infirm preferred to struggle for survival outside the poorhouses.

Owen categorized his era as "the age of great discoveries, and of much competition."[3] He attributed deteriorating standards of human conduct—the excessive zeal for the acquisition of wealth, too often without regard for the interests of others, the extremely competitive spirit spreading throughout the nation, and the exploitation of the working class—to the rapid changes wrought by the Industrial Revolution. He pointed out that people have always been conditioned by circumstances, that the pressures of new economic forces were damaging the attitudes and behavior patterns of the nation. Since the sole or at least dominant objective of com-

merce was now "immediate pecuniary gain,"[4] the intense ambition
thus engendered to achieve success and amass wealth encouraged
deceptive practices and widespread chicanery. Industrialization,
said Owen, was destroying the time-honored high standards and
traditions of business. He firmly attributed such a deterioration of
character, not to individuals as such, but to the economic system.

III Children in the New Industrial Society

Children were among the most unfortunate victims of the new industrial society. Those who survived the high infant mortality rate,
often suffered through a wretched childhood. Many parents, to obtain more income, sent their children (girls as well as boys) as young
as six years of age to work in crowded, poorly ventilated, overheated
mills or factories. The hours of work were overlong—Owen noted
that the usual workday began at 6 A.M. and ended at 8 P.M., with
only one hour of rest during the day—[5] the pay was low, and the
machinery dangerous. In many factories children were required to
stand on their feet all day while working at their machines. Often
meals, which were supposedly provided by the factory owners, were
forgotten, or were brought to the children to be consumed as they
worked. Usually the quality of the meals was poor and the quantity
insufficient. If the children attended night school, they were
generally too fatigued to learn much. Factory foremen, in many
cases dependent upon the output for their wages, commonly kept
them working at a brisk pace by applying the rod or whip.
Overwork, lack of sanitation, and malnutrition subjected them to
serious, sometimes fatal, illnesses. The accident rate mounted owing
to lack of protection from unsafe machines, which frequently
mutilated the young workers' arms or legs. Fever epidemics broke
out in the factory towns. Medical help was not available to the poor
in most places in the late eighteenth century, and even when such
attention was available, the state of medical science was so
rudimentary as to make it of limited value to the patient.

Children were in great demand as factory workers, not only
because their labor was cheap, but also because their thin fingers
made it easy for them to clean the machines. Some manufacturers
hired children out of the orphanages and set them to work for paltry
wages or none at all. Since there were no laws regulating child

labor, these young victims remained entirely at the mercy of their self-centered employers.

In 1802 Parliament enacted the first law in Britain to regulate child labor, namely, the Health and Morals of Apprentices Act, which, however, protected only the parish apprentices, that is, children in the care of charitable institutions. The law required that proper ventilation must be provided in all factories, that walls and ceilings of workshops must be whitewashed at least twice each year, that apprentices must not allowed to work more than twelve hours daily, and that girls must be housed separately from boys. This act of Parliament, even though not prescribing any uniform system of enforcing its provisions, made a significant beginning in the struggle for state regulation of working conditions.

IV *Owen's Reformist Proposals*

Owen had mastered and expertly utilized the new methods of production in order to become a successful businessman. He won fame as a captain of industry, but he had more important goals in mind. From the earliest days of his success he gave intensive thought to the problem of reforming the living and working conditions of the common people. He intended to create a rational system to replace the disordered one that accompanied the Industrial Revolution.

He attributed the misfortune of the lower orders to the greed of the upper classes. The thirst for luxuries, he said, had "generated a disposition which strongly impels its possessors to sacrifice the best feelings of human nature to this love of accumulation."[6] In his view, the exploitation of workers, whom the industrialists regarded as "instruments of gain,"[7] was the inevitable result of too rapid industrialization.

In 1803 Owen became a member of the Committee of Management of the board representing the cotton industry and took an active part in seeking to alleviate the economic and social problems confronting the industry. In 1815 he called a meeting of Scottish manufacturers to consider asking the government to rescind the tax on cotton imports and to discuss the plight of children and older workers in the textile factories.

At this time he advocated, in addition to tax abatement, several specific measures for the benefit of employees: (1) exclusion of children under twelve years of age from work in the factories; (2) shortening of the workday to a maximum of twelve hours, which would include ninety minutes to be allowed for meals; and (3) administration of educational tests to prospective employees, who would not be hired unless they had mastered the fundamentals of reading, writing, and arithmetic. He noted that these ideas were not really new, for thirty years previously children under fourteen were not expected to go to work,[8] and the workday was limited to a maximum of twelve hours. Good working conditions meant happier, more efficient employees. Owen suggested that his proposals would be beneficial "to the child, to the parent, to the employer, and to the country."[9] Convincing other businessmen was no simple task, however; all the other manufacturers agreed to the lowering of taxes, but none favored the improvement of conditions in their factories.

Nonetheless, undaunted by negative reactions to his ideas, Owen persisted until he prevailed upon Sir Robert Peel to sponsor a bill in Parliament for the relief of working children. That bill, a modified version of Owen's original proposals, contained the following provisions: (1) children under ten would not be hired for work in factories; (2) employees under eighteen would have a maximum workday of 12.5 hours, including half an hour for instruction in elementary school subjects; and (3) inspectors would be appointed to enforce the new regulations. In 1816 Owen appeared before a parliamentary committee to testify about working conditions in the factories. Two years later his bill passed in the House of Commons but failed to pass in the House of Lords, which was reluctant to interfere in matters involving the relationship between parent and child. Another factor contributing to the defeat of the bill was the fear that if the workday was shortened the lower class might misuse its idle hours.

After further investigation, in 1819 the House of Lords reversed its decision and passed the bill under the title, First Factory Act. This legislation, although largely ineffective because it failed to provide for the appointment of inspectors to enforce it (a provision in the original bill defeated in 1818), was important in that the state for the first time accepted responsibility for the protection of civil rights. (The more limited law of 1802 applied only to parish apprentices, and did not restrict very young children from working.) The state, intervening as a guardian of all children, now prescribed conditions of their employment, a precedent which paved the way for more effective, far-reaching measures to be enacted during the 1830s.

V *Proposals for Poor Relief*

In addition to his active role in improving working conditions in the factories, Owen had become involved in promoting relief for the poor. In 1815 in England the end of the European wars resulted in grave economic distress, unemployment, overproduction, and the devaluation of goods. Owen attributed the distress to

the new extraordinary changes which had occurred during so long a war, when men and materials had been for a quarter of a century in such urgent demand, to support the waste of our armies and navies upon so extensive a scale for so long a period. All things had attained to war prices, and these had been so long maintained, that they had appeared to the present generation the natural state of business and public affairs. The want of hands and materials, with this lavish expenditure, created a demand for and gave great encouragement to new mechanical inventions and chemical discoveries, to supersede manual labour in supplying the materials required for warlike purposes, and these, direct and indirect, were innumerable. The war was a great and most extravagant customer to farmers, manufacturers, and other producers of wealth, and many during this period became very wealthy.[10]

As long as the war continued, businessmen prospered. However, when the war came to an end, Owen said,

this great customer of the producers died, and prices fell as the demand diminished, until the *prime cost* of the articles required for war could not be obtained. The barns and farmyards were full, warehouses loaded, and such was our artificial state of society, that this very superabundance of wealth was the sole cause of the existing distress. Burn the stock in the farmyards and warehouses, and prosperity would immediately recommence in the same manner as if the war had continued.[11]

Men returning from the army and navy found that there were no jobs waiting for them, as often happens to veterans today; in many cases there were no jobs because new or improved machines could be used to do the work—and at lower cost.

In 1816 Owen had addressed the Association for the Relief of the Manufacturing and Laboring Poor, and its president, the Duke of York, showed definite interest in Owen's views on poor relief. In 1817, discussing the problem with a Select Committee of the House of Commons on the Poor Laws, Owen expressed his conviction that the difficulties of the poor resulted from the "depreciation of human labour"[12] attributable to the introduction of machines into the factories. As long as work had been done by manpower, supply and demand had remained in correct proportion to one another; when machines replaced manual labor, overproduction resulted. Working people lost prestige and their labor was inevitably valued less as machinery became more highly developed. "The steam engine and spinning machines, with the endless mechanical inventions to which they have given rise have, however, inflicted evils on society which now greatly over-balance the benefits which are derived from them."[13] Machines had, Owen felt, widened the gulf between the rich and the poor, making a few men unjustifiably rich at the expense of their workers. Discussing a major issue of his time, currency reform, Owen advocated the use of labor notes instead of gold or silver or paper currency, which he considered to be artificial. Since human labor created wealth, the worker should receive payment in proportion to the amount of work done. In this way the producers would benefit from their labor, and the working class would be freed from exploitation by other classes. Owen's plan for currency reform was later revised and put into practice in his labor exchanges.

Since it was unacceptable to let the poor starve and unlikely that industrialists would use fewer machines in order to create more jobs for the underprivileged, Owen concluded that some new form of practical assistance to the poor should be devised, and that satisfactory work opportunities for them should be found. He suggested that Parliament pass an act nationalizing the poor. It was the duty of government, he believed, to educate the poor and to create employment for them, preferably in agricultural and manufacturing villages or, alternatively, in work on roads, canals, harbors, and ships. Such a plan was intended to alleviate the distress of the poor and to benefit all of society. He felt that "every part of society would be essentially benefited by this change in the condition of the poor."[14]

Owen advocated that instruction should be provided for the children of the poor, an innovation since it had not been customary for poor children to attend school. He proposed the organization of self-sufficient communities based on socialist principles. He envisioned subdivisions occupying plots of land of 1,000 to 1,500 acres neatly laid out like parallelograms, each accommodating about twelve hundred people, with dormitories and schools for children three years of age or older. Such communities should ideally be built by the government; yet, if the government refused to acknowledge its duty to the poor, communities might be initiated by "individuals,—by parishes,—by counties,—by districts."[15] Building communities would be no problem, Owen reasoned, because all things necessary for the development of the communities were easily attainable in England. "Nothing new would be required; all that could be wanted is in daily practice all over this kingdom."[16]

Owen believed that his proposed villages would provide numerous advantages not available in the existing manufacturing towns. In August 1817, he made public his views comparing the conditions in manufacturing towns with those that would prevail in his new villages:

In the Manufacturing Towns

The poor and working classes now usually live in garrets or cellars, within narrow lanes or confined courts.

They are surrounded with dirt, enveloped in smoke, and they have seldom a pleasant object on which to fix their eye.

In the Proposed Villages

The poor and working classes will live in dwellings formed into a large square, rendered in every way convenient, and usefully ornamented.

They will be surrounded by gardens, have abundance of space in all directions to keep the air healthy and pleasant, they will have walks and plantations before them, within the square, and well cultivated grounds, kept in good order, around, as far as the eye can reach.

Parents are oppressed with anxiety to secure the means of subsistence for themselves and children.

In consequence of the principle of mutual co-operation being understood and practised to its full extent, the necessaries and comforts of life are enjoyed by all in abundance.

Each family must have domestic arrangements for cooking, &c., and one person must be wholly occupied in preparing provisions, &c. for a family of ordinary numbers.

The best provisions will be cooked in the best manner under arrangements that will enable five or six individuals to prepare provisions for 1,000.

The parents must toil from 10 to 16 hours in the day, to procure the wretched subsistence which they obtain for themselves and children, and very often under circumstances the most unfavourable to health and natural enjoyments.

The parents will be healthfully and pleasantly occupied not more than eight hours in the day.

In bad times, and which frequently occur, the parties experience a distress not easily to be described.

Under the arrangements proposed no bad times can occur from a change of markets, or from any commercial uncertainties, as the parties will always have a plentiful stock of all things necessary.

In cases of sickness, every evil takes place among these individualized beings.

In the event of sickness the utmost attention and care will be experienced; every one, both from principle and interest, will be active and have pleasure in rendering the situation of the invalid as comfortable as possible.

The early death of parents leave the children orphans and subject to every evil.

The early death of parents leave the children in all respects well provided and protected.

The children are usually sickly, and, as well as their parents, ill-clothed.

The children will be ruddy and healthy, and, as well as their parents, neat, clean, and properly clothed.

The young children are much neglected, and hourly acquire bad habits.

The children will be well looked after, prevented from acquiring bad, and taught good, habits.

The education of the children neglected.	The children all well trained and well informed.
The children sent early in life to some one trade or manufacture, usually of a very unhealthy nature, and at which they must attend from 10 to 16 hours per day.	The children gradually instructed in gardening, agriculture, and some trade or manufacture, and only employed according to age and strength.
The children trained under ignorant persons, possessing many bad habits.	The children will be trained by intelligent persons, possessing only good habits.
Scolding, coercion, and punishments are the usual instruments of training here.	But here kindness and good sense will be the only instruments of training.

To proceed with the contrast would be endless; the mind of the reader will easily supply the remainder; suffice it therefore to say,—

That this—is the abode of poverty, vice, crime, and misery.	While this will ever be the abode of abundance, active intelligence, correct conduct, and happiness.[17]

Owen regarded physical comfort and freedom from want as prerequisites for the betterment of mankind. He predicted that

the means provided in these establishments, will give every stimulus to bring forth and to perfect the best parts only of every character, by furnishing inhabitants with such valuable instruction as they could not acquire by any other means, and by affording sufficient leisure and freedom from anxiety to promote the natural direction of their powers: when thus prepared by early imbibed temperate habits, by an accurate knowledge of facts, and by a full conviction that their efforts are directed for the benefit of mankind, it is not easy to imagine, with our present ideas, what may be accomplished by human beings so trained and so circumstanced.[18]

He condemned the existing methods of poor relief because they rewarded "idleness and vice" and perpetuated "the degradation and misery of the classes whom they are designed to serve" instead of rewarding "industry and virtue"[19] as his proposed system of workers' communities would do. He argued that the new system would benefit not only the poor by raising their standard of living and improving their behavior patterns, but all other classes and the nation as a whole. He estimated that his program of poor relief would cost about £96,000 per subdivision to set up but would probably, within a single generation, eliminate all need for contributions to charity. "Expensive as such a system for the unemployed poor may appear to a superficial observer, it will be found, on mature investigation by those who understand all the consequences of such a combination, to be by far the most economical that has yet been devised."[20] Owen worked out the following calculations:

SCHEDULE *of* EXPENSES *for forming an Establishment for*
1,200 MEN, WOMEN, AND CHILDREN.[21]

If the land be purchased,

1,200 acres of land, at £30, per acre	£36,000
Lodging apartments for 1,200 persons	17,000
Three public buildings within the square	11,000
Manufactory, slaughter-house, and washing house	8,000
Furnishing 300 lodging-rooms, at £8 each	2,400
Furnishing kitchen, schools, and dormitories	3,000
Two farming establishments, with corn-mill, and malting and brewing appendages	5,000
Making the interior of the square and roads	3,000
Stock for the farm under spade cultivation	4,000
Contingencies and extras	6,600
	£96,000

Dividing this sum by 1,200 residents, Owen arrived at the conclusion that on a per capita basis the capital required would be small. Furthermore, if the community were to be built on rented land, only £60,000, would be needed.

He converted many influential people to his schemes, yet predictably those most attracted to his plans were the poor. Although initially they were irritated by Owen's paternalistic manner and disapproval of their behavior, so that in 1817 at two public meetings they voted against his proposals for unemployment, eventually many responded favorably. The security and comfort promised by Owen naturally appealed to those who struggled for their daily necessities. A contemporary member of the working class, William

Lovett, who became a leader of the Chartist reform movement, said:

Community of property . . . has a peculiar attraction for the plodding, toiling, ill remunerated sons and daughters of labour. The idea of all the powers of machinery, of all the arts and inventions of men, being applied for the benefit of all in common, to the lightening of their toil and the increase of their comforts, is the most captivating to those who accept the idea without investigation. The prospect of having spacious halls, gardens, libraries, and museums at their command; of having light alternate labour in field or factory; of seeing their children educated, provided and cared for at the public expense; of having no fear or care of poverty themselves; nor for wife, children, or friends they might leave behind them; is one of the most cheering and consolatory to an enthusiastic mind.[22]

Owen countered the arguments of those who thought that this new army of laborers would cause overproduction of agricultural and manufacturing commodities by asking, "Is it possible that there can be too many productions desirable and useful to society?"[23] To those who feared declining property values in communal villages Owen responded that the improvements made upon hitherto neglected land would undoubtedly increase the value of the communities and the surrounding areas: "The land and houses would not only possess their original worth, but as the plan advanced, both would materially increase in value; and all the districts in the neighbourhood of these communities would partake of the general amelioration which they could not fail to introduce in a very extensive degree."[24]

But the main achievement of Owen's proposed system would be to reeducate the poor in terms of moral behavior and rational knowledge. Owen proposed to eradicate the selfish behavior which then motivated his fellow countrymen. Communal living and cooperative production would foster new social relationships.

Under the present system there is the most minute division of mental power and manual labour in the individuals of the working classes; private interests are placed perpetually at variance with the public good; and in every nation men are purposely trained from infancy to suppose that their well-being is incompatible with the progress and prosperity of other nations. Such are the means by which old society seeks to obtain the desired

objects of life. The details now to be submitted have been devised upon
principles which will lead to an opposite practice; to the combination of extensive mental and manual powers in the individuals of the working classes;
to a complete identity of private and public interest; and to the training of
nations to comprehend that their power and happiness cannot attain their
full and natural development but through an equal increase of the power
and happiness of all other states.[25]

In order to advance his proposed reforms, Owen twice became a
candidate for a seat in Parliament. He had previously considered
entering politics but had lost an opportunity to stand for Parliament
owing to the pressure of business at a time when the "thought of
being a candidate in reality never entered my mind."[26] Later he
said regretfully that he would certainly have been elected if he had
hurried home from a business journey to campaign. He made a
serious effort to win the election of 1819 but met with defeat which
he attributed to bribery of voters by his opponent. He was defeated
again in 1847 when he ran on a platform setting forth drastic
reforms characterized by a contemporary observer as far "in advance of his times."[27] His platform contained the following nine
planks, most of them destined to become accepted doctrines of
modern democracies:

1. A graduated property tax equal to the national expenditure.
2. The abolition of all other taxes.
3. No taxation without representation.
4. Free trade with all the world.
5. National education for all who desire it.
6. National beneficial employment for all who require it.
7. Full and complete freedom of religion under every name by which men
   may call themselves.
8. A national circulating medium, under the supervision and control of
   Parliament, that could be increased or diminished as wealth for circulation increased or diminished; and that should be, by its ample security,
   unchangeable in its value.
9. National military training for all male children in schools, that the
   country may be protected against foreign invasion, without the present
   heavy permanent military expenditure.[28]

In contrast to the materialistic, reactionary leaders of British industry and government at that time, Owen agitated for a peaceful

form of social revolution to educate the masses, improve their working and living conditions, and achieve a more humane, cooperative society.

Although Owen's socialism did not win favor immediately, when Owen returned from America in 1828 he found the British workers had adopted many of his proposals, making him the leader of a movement for labor rights. Some of Owen's disciples adapted and developed certain of his proposals into successful agitation for social change. Many political and social reforms that were effected in Britain in the mid to late nineteenth century owe much to Owen's early socialist doctrines.

Owen's proposals differed from later socialist and communist programs in many ways. First, Owen was concerned not only with the economic well-being of the laborers, but also with their morality, behavior, and intellect. Second, Owen first formulated his theories at a time when the working class had no real cohesiveness. He thought of himself as a benefactor of the poor and did not think in terms of class unity. Third, in Owen's time the concept of government being responsible for the welfare of its citizens had not yet been developed. Therefore his assertions that the government must find useful employment for the poor were viewed with suspicion. Since the government was not thought to be responsible for the welfare of its citizens, Owen did not believe that the government necessarily had to be involved in his schemes, but rather that his plans could be effected by any charitable group. Generally thought of as a utopian socialist, Owen had an idyllic vision of a peacefully changed world. He did not believe in revolution or radical organizations of any kind.

Frederick Engels (co-author with Karl Marx of the *Communist Manifesto*) ascribed the origins of social reform in Great Britain to Owen's efforts:

Every social movement, every real advance in England on behalf of the workers links itself on to the name of Robert Owen. He forced through in 1819, after five years' fighting, the first law limiting the hours of labor of women and children in factories. He was president of the first Congress at which all the Trade Unions of England united in a single great trade association. He introduced as transition measures to the complete communistic organization of society, on the one hand, co-operative societies for retail trade and production. . . . On the other hand, he introduced labor bazaars for the exchange of the products of labor through the medium of labor-notes, whose unit was a single hour of work; . . . [these institutions] did not claim to be the panacea for all social ills, but only a first step towards a much more radical revolution of society.[29]

Owen's proposals for the drastic reform of society through cooperative communities earned for him his reputation as the first great British socialist.

CHAPTER 3

Owen's Philosophy of Education

PROFOUNDLY disturbed by the mounting evils accompanying the Industrial Revolution—the tragic impact of oppressive working conditions upon family life, the deterioration of body and mind attributable to epidemics of disease, accidents in the factories and mills, and particularly the treadmill-like, barren existence of the poor—Owen concluded that far-reaching social reform was imperative. He could think of only one feasible means of effecting such reform, namely, good, universal education which the government had the obligation and power to make available.

His philosophy of education stemmed from a firm conviction that man can readily control and change environmental conditions and forces which decisively influence human nature and conduct. He believed that the creation of a favorable environment would result in a desirable national character. The best way to achieve this end, Owen came to believe, would be to organize controlled communities from which all unfavorable influences would be removed so that ethical character would be molded in accordance with carefully planned specifications.

I Social Aims of Education

Owen was interested in education, not as a method of academic instruction but primarily as a means of achieving social reform. For this reason his educational philosophy emphasized the community rather than the individual; the education of the latter seemed important only insofar as it reshaped the character of the community as a whole; and, furthermore, he broadened the scope of his interest until by 1812 he had gone so far as to conclude that reeducating single communities was important only if that process helped to create a morally superior nation. Eventually he extended his educational aims to include the interests of all humanity, the remaking of human nature on a worldwide basis.

The first essential step in the drastic reform of society, said Owen, must be to educate young children in such a way that they will develop desirable attitudes and habits before maturity. Education for social reform should begin with children because they are more malleable than adults, whose character traits have become relatively fixed and difficult to change. Owen insisted that, although anyone, young or old, can be taught to conform to acceptable behavior patterns, such training is much easier to provide effectively if started at an early age before the person has formed persistent bad habits. He asserted that an orderly, more humane society could readily be created by teaching every young person to conduct himself in a socially approved manner. "It must be obvious upon reflection that a human being well-trained and educated from birth, physically, intellectually, morally, and practically, will be a far more valuable product to the world than one entirely neglected in these respects or ill-educated in all or any of them."[1]

Owen hoped "to improve the breed of men, more than men have yet improved the breed of domestic animals."[2] It was his view that, since the future of the human race depended upon the correct method of rearing children, they should be

trained systematically to acquire useful knowledge through the means of sensible signs, by which their powers of reflection and judgment may be habituated to draw accurate conclusions from the facts presented to them. This mode of instruction is founded in nature, and will supersede the present defective and tiresome system of book learning, which is ill calculated to give either pleasure or instruction to the minds of children.[3]

Learning through meaningful experiences and attractively presented lessons would, Owen suggested, make education more interesting to children and could conceivably increase the pupils' attention spans and learning rates. Since learning would thus become an asset desired by the children themselves, they would not only derive the benefits of formal instruction but also simultaneously acquire good habits and a cheerful disposition. Education would no longer be a chore. Children would willingly undergo training in the skills necessary for the preservation and well-being of society.

Owen had no doubt that these cooperative children would become happy adults and that society would soon be transformed into a community of contented citizens.

He described the potential results of his proposed educational program as follows:

Not a few individuals only, but the whole population of the world, may in a few years be rendered a very far superior race of beings to any now upon the earth, or which has been made known to us by history.[4]

He asserted that the human race, if it adhered to his plan, could within one generation fulfill its highest aspirations and develop its fullest powers—all by means of gradual, peaceful social change. He predicted that man would eventually, by adhering to those same principles, reach the millenium, that age of perfection when society would be totally free of vice, crime, and poverty, and government would no longer be necessary.

II *Character Education*

Should the individual be held responsible for the development of his own character and behavior patterns? Owen's autobiography answered this question succinctly: "The character of each of our race is formed by God or nature and by society; . . . it is impossible that any human being could or can form his own qualities or character."[5]

Although he admitted the presence of some innate qualities, Owen maintained that character is formed by the environment, never significantly by heredity, and he concluded that each person's character could be reshaped in any desirable way, that the only things needed to develop any given personality would be the right kind of educational programs and properly trained adults to administer it. He rejected the prevalent assumptions that man is responsible for his own behavior and that only punishment or the threat of punishment can deter a person from carrying out evil impulses. On the contrary, he believed that preventive measures for the inculcation of approved character traits are essential inasmuch as punishment of the individual after he has formed persistent bad habits is useless. His educational philosophy and theories of social reform were based upon the conviction that:

Any general character, from the best to the worst, from the most ignorant to the most enlightened, may be given to any community, even to the world at large, by the application of proper means; which means are to a great extent at the command and under the control of those who have influence in the affairs of men.[6]

As he reflected upon his own life experience, Owen concluded that nature had provided him with certain fundamental traits or qualities while society had imposed upon him a particular language, religion, and mode of behavior. He was therefore the product of both nature and nurture. Since neither he nor any other human being had ever been free to choose his own character, this choice must be made by society, which can easily train children along socially desirable lines. A program such as the one he had espoused for effective education and social reform would eliminate all social evils and create a permanently happy society of competent, cooperative citizens.

By my own experience and reflection I had ascertained that human nature is radically good, and is capable of being trained, educated, and placed from birth in such manner, that all ultimately (that is, as soon as the gross errors and corruptions of the present false and wicked system are overcome and destroyed) must become united, good, wise, wealthy, and happy.[7]

To eradicate the defects in human character, said Owen, it is necessary only to teach the child desired attitudes and habits at a very early age. This optimistic view of man's original nature (and potential development) contradicted the Christian doctrine that man is born a sinner. If the latter view that man is basically evil were accepted, then, in Owen's judgment, society would have to devise safeguards to protect itself from him. Owen regarded man as neither good nor bad at birth, but capable of developing qualities in either direction, depending upon the behavior patterns of the society in which he is reared.

He felt confident that his proposed educational programs would encounter no formidable difficulties which might impede the process of instilling in the human race the knowledge and character he considered essential to the happiness of all mankind.

As all men are born ignorant and inexperienced, and must receive their knowledge, either from the instincts of their nature, which are given to them at their birth, or from surrounding external objects, animate and inanimate, which they do not create; all, by nature have equal rights.[8]

The man-made inequities of society seemed highly unjust to Owen in the light of his belief that all people have become what they are only because of the particular circumstances into which they were born. They could learn the same good behavior patterns displayed by anyone else in the community if provided with equal opportunities and rights.

Owen planned to establish at New Lanark a school in which appropriate modes of behavior, in addition to the traditional curriculum, would be taught both to children and to adults. He became so confident and enthusiastic about his proposed system of teaching ethical conduct and guiding people to develop fine character traits that he expected immediate approval by everyone who heard about its aims and methods. His entire career was marred by the inability to accept the fact that many people familiar with his system did not embrace it. Throughout his lifetime he expected his educational and social reforms to win adherents around the world. He felt certain that New Lanark would become a model for all future societies, and he rejected any possibility that society, after being fully apprised of his theories, might still not change for the better. Surely, he thought, as the new knowledge he was providing spread among the people, no one would be in opposition, and there would be "no conceivable foundation for private displeasure or public enmity."[9] "Let the authorities of this age now turn their attention to this subject, and they will discover that they have attained the knowledge of a moral lever by which they can with ease remove ignorance, poverty, disunion, vice, crime, evil passions, and misery from mankind. Place the human race from birth within superior spiritual and material surroundings, and the evils and sufferings of humanity will be no longer experienced, and will be retained on record only to enhance the pleasures of this new existence for man."[10]

III *Reeducation of Adults*

Owen had anticipated one of the main obstacles to his educational and social reforms, namely, the fact that adults, the very people whose duty it would be to teach desirable attitudes and habits to children, had not generally developed these character traits themselves, owing to negligent or erroneous instruction by their own parents. It seemed to him deplorable that adults did not seem to possess the qualities of character essential to the initiation and effective implementation of his system. Many of them had been educated in a rigid fashion, with primary emphasis upon rote memorization; others had been instructed in half-truths or in false information; and still others had received no education at all, making them the least likely to develop good character in children.

The bad example of adults would make it difficult or even impossible to obtain permanent results with children continuously exposed to undesirable influences of this kind. Owen insisted on the necessity for reeducating adults while at the same time separating impressionable children from them for as much of the day as expedient.[11] Thus, during brief periods of reunion with their children, parents could show them love and devotion but would have little opportunity to lead them astray through ill-conceived training or display of unworthy character traits.

Noting that a generation gap would arise if children developed much better behavior patterns than their parents, Owen contemplated methods of adult education to close this gap. Adults would have to be reeducated to become good citizens, models for their children to emulate. He felt certain that mature people, as soon as they were informed about their own shortcomings (and he would so inform them so that they would see themselves clearly as in a mirror), would be eager to become superior human beings and attain the state of moral perfection envisioned for his new society.

Owen still gave priority to the training of children because they have not yet formed rigid character traits and are plastic enough to be easily guided in the right direction. Moreover, he emphasized the fact that children, soon to be the next generation of adults, provided the only prospect of fulfilling his dream—the creation of a new, morally superior, rational society. If he could achieve hoped for results in working with the present generation of children, despite the adverse influence of their parents and teachers, themselves products of a morally imperfect society, he would have no fear about future generations, for they would be well prepared to participate in the rational social system he proposed to establish. He wanted most of all to instill in the young those characteristics which he called "rational habits," among them order, temperance, industry, honesty, and regularity. The development of these habits, he urged, should precede all formal education; he was confident that children properly trained to conform to high standards of conduct would never harbor ill-will toward others and would be inclined to practice cooperation and mutual aid.

He felt sure that he would eventually succeed in motivating adults to change their behavior and way of life in order to attain their primary goal, happiness. Man forever strives, he believed, to achieve this secret goal, for, "it appears to be an universal law of Nature or of God, that all life, in whatever form or organization it may appear, desires to be happy; or, in other words, that, by its natural instinct, it continually makes every effort in its power to avoid or be relieved from pain, and to attain the enjoyment, according to its individual nature or organization, of agreeable and pleasurable sensations. . . . This is the secret motive or instinct to all physical or mental movements in each individual of the human race."[12]

Owen enumerated thirteen conditions that he believed to be prerequisite to the achievement of happiness:

1st. The possession of a good organization, physical, mental, and moral.
2nd. The power of procuring at pleasure whatever is necessary to preserve the organization in the best state of health.
3rd. The best education, from birth to maturity, of the physical, intellectual, and moral powers, of all the population.
4th. The inclination and means of promoting continually the happiness of our fellow-beings.
5th. The inclination and means of continually increasing our stock of knowledge.
6th. The power of enjoying the best society; and more especially of associating at pleasure with those for whom we are compelled to feel the most regard and greatest affection.
7th. The means of travelling at pleasure.
8th. The absence of superstitution, supernatural fears, and the fear of death.
9th. Full liberty of expressing our thoughts upon all subjects.
10th. The utmost individual freedom of action, compatible with the permanent good of society.

11th. To have the character formed for us to express the truth upon all oc-
       casions, and to have pure charity for the feelings, thoughts, and con-
       duct, of all mankind, and a sincere good will for every individual of
       the human race.

12th. To reside in a society, whose laws, institutions, and arrangements,
       well organized, and well governed, are all in unison with the laws of
       human nature. And

Lastly, to know that all that have life are as happy as their natures will
admit, but especially all of the human race.[13]

But no one could remain truly happy in a world afflicted by
widespread poverty, crime, and suffering. Even very young
children, he insisted, can be taught the lesson that bringing happiness to others is the only way to achieve happiness for themselves.
Children so educated will as adults eagerly participate in the
perpetual search for universal happiness and will follow the rational
way of life calculated to advance that greatest goal of mankind.

Happiness is, after all, "the object of all human exertions."[14]
Happiness, according to Owen, would be fully realized when "all
men possess health, real knowledge, and wealth."[15] But, in preparation for the new state of happiness, man must be reeducated.

Before man could be wise and happy, his mind must be born again—that is,
it must be discharged of all the inconsistent associations which have been
formed within it; the foundation must be laid anew, and a superstructure
raised of just and useful proportions, consistent in each and in all its parts,
and such as shall please, gratify, and delight the eye of all beholders; that
shall bear the test of the most scientific investigations; that, through all
future ages, shall satisfy each mind as it advances, well trained and formed,
to maturity, that it is the abode of happiness proceeding from correct conduct, under the guidance of the best intelligence and the soundest
wisdom![16]

Ultimately, said Owen, all human beings will realize that happiness for oneself can be secured only in a society which gives the
highest priority to the happiness of each and every individual: "The
happiness of self, clearly understood and uniformly practised . . .
can only be attained by conduct that must promote the happiness of
the community."[17]

He rejected the idea that the poor should be held accountable for
their plight. On the contrary, he displayed a paternalistic attitude

toward them, advocating that they be provided with adequate training so that they might cope better with their sad condition. Their imperfect character traits and incapacities should be attributed, he declared, not to themselves but to the social system which deprived them of opportunity and caused their personality defects and predicament. It seemed unjust to blame the lower classes, even the criminals in them, for such tragic consequences of an imperfect society as vice, crime, and poverty. The environment molds people, makes them what they become, said Owen, and an adverse environment must be remedied so that none will be poor and all will be cooperative, prosperous, worthy, and efficient citizens.

Not only the poor, but also the well-to-do, the British upper classes, had developed in childhood undesirable character traits requiring drastic remedial measures. Owen noted that many of these affluent people had been reared by ignorant, lower-class servants from whom they had learned bad habits and false ideas. With the advent of industrialization, more and more adults in the lower classes found few opportunities for employment in production and applied for jobs as domestics, work for which they were poorly qualified since they brought to it the mischievous habits transmitted in their own homes from one generation to the next. To these untrained domestics many in the upper classes entrusted the upbringing of their sons and daughters who would become the leaders of society and merely pass on the same false teachings and bad examples to children in an endless chain.

Owen stressed the urgent need for adult education: "It is indeed impossible that children in any situation can be correctly trained, until those who surround them from infancy shall be previously well-instructed."[18] On the other hand, he also concluded that, with enough effort and good educational programs, well-trained teachers could be successful with many children despite the bad influence of adults.

Human nature, save the minute differences which are ever found in all the compounds of the creation, is one and the same in all; it is without exception universally plastic, and by judiciously training *the infants of any one class in the world may be readily formed into men of any other class, even to believe and declare that conduct to be right and virtuous, and to die in its defence, which their parents had been taught to believe and say was wrong and vicious, and to oppose which, those parents would also have willingly sacrificed their lives.*[19]

Note the emphasis upon the plasticity of human nature and the need for judicious training of children which is to be accomplished by providing a wholesome environment conducive to their mental and physical development. The process of education should ideally be continuous, not restricted to school hours, so that each new generation would learn good habits from adult models and from their total life experiences.

In his search for an environment most favorable to an ideal education, Owen initiated experiments in cooperative living, the first of which was the democratically run New Lanark community where every adult had a vote on all decisions affecting the community while Owen himself served as paternalistic benefactor and leader.

IV   A New View of Society

In *A New View of Society,*[20] a book of essays Owen published in 1813 and circulated among influential people to win their support for his ideas, he made certain statements about human nature which he regarded as irrefutable axioms. It seemed to him that all those statements followed logically from one to the next and together constituted a self-evident social theory. He began with the truism that man is born with a desire to satisfy basic needs and thereby attain happiness. All human beings, therefore, always do whatever will bring them the greatest possible satisfaction. In other words, self-interest motivates all of man's actions. He then pointed out that man is born with "animal propensities" (driving impulses) which stimulate the desire to sustain, enjoy, and propagate life. He strives to maintain and prolong life and to perpetuate it through the birth of his children.

Owen divided the attributes of human nature into two classes: the innate and the acquired. Man is endowed at birth with faculties which, almost from that moment onward until death, enable him to receive, exchange, and evaluate ideas. The mind, the faculties, the animal propensities, and the desire for happiness are all formed in the womb as innate equipment. These characteristics of human nature, therefore, cannot be determined by the individual who possesses them, Yet, the mind matures and strengthens itself with age. Each person's mind differs from that of others, thereby making possible the diversity of talents, interests, and abilities which is present in every generation. But only a few basic tendencies have been formed before birth; all other qualities of human nature are developed subsequently during the course of life experience.

Man's knowledge is derived from his environment. He learns by imitating the behavior patterns of his elders and obtaining instruction from them. Knowledge possessed by an individual may be narrow or broad, false or true, depending on the education he has received as a child, but, however that may be, his happiness must always depend on whatever knowledge he has acquired. He will be happy in proportion to the correct knowledge he and those around him possess. He cannot achieve true happiness if he and his associates make decisions based upon faulty or incomplete knowledge.

Owen believed, and tried through his experiments to prove, that all people could experience perfect happiness if they would only accumulate a maximum of knowledge within the limits of their capacities. In order to attain such happiness they must be taught to distinguish truth from error and to cultivate their ability to reason.[21] He reiterated his faith in the power of knowledge to remake human nature:

. . . in proportion as man's desire of self-happiness, or his self-love, is directed by true knowledge, those actions will abound which are virtuous and beneficial to man; . . . in proportion as it is influenced by false notions, or the absence of true knowledge, those actions will prevail which generate crimes, from whence arises an endless variety of misery; and, consequently, . . . every rational means should be now adopted to detect error, and to increase true knowledge among men.

. . . when these truths are made evident, every individual will necessarily endeavour to promote the happiness of every other individual within his sphere of action, because he must clearly, and without any doubt, comprehend such conduct to be the essence of self-interest or true cause of self-happiness.[22]

Changes that should be made in the kind and amount of

knowledge imparted to individuals would alter their character for the better and thereby transform their entire society. Owen declared that his proposed educational and social reforms would result in peaceful change of revolutionary proportions throughout the world and would eradicate all evils that stand in the way of universal happiness. Violence would be of no use for building a better world, for the necessary changes must be made within the individual before improvements in external conditions can be achieved: "The change from the ignorant, repulsive, unorganized, and miserable present, to the enlightened, attractive, organized, and happy future, can never be effected by violence, or through feelings of anger and ill-will to any portion of mankind."[23] The only means of progress, said Owen, is understanding, by which he meant adherence to "great fundamental truths . . . peace, kindness, . . . charity, . . . patience and perseverance."[24] Owen himself was a model of perseverance in his opinions and unmoveability in his beliefs.

Owen expected his new system of education to result in a brotherhood of man. The newly trained man's "heart will be open to receive, and his hand ready to assist, each of his fellow creatures, whatever may be his sect, his class, his party, his country, or his colour. Anger, hatred, and revenge will have no place on which to rest; the pabulum on which all the evil passions fed will no longer exist; unity and mutual co-operation to any extent will become easy of execution and the common practise of all."[25]

So convinced was he of the validity of his theories that he could not imagine how any human being motivated, as all people are, by self-interest could fail to act in the suggested way—the way that would bring happiness to those around him who, in turn, would act with similar kindness toward others so that all would reap the rewards of exemplary behavior. In a sense, Owen was merely elaborating upon the Golden Rule. If each person would act in a beneficent manner in relation to fellow human beings, they would reciprocate with equal goodwill in order that he, too, might attain personal happiness. To fulfill his basic goal of achieving happiness, the individual must devote himself to the happiness of others.

CHAPTER 4

Social Reforms at New Lanark

W HEN Robert Owen assumed the directorship of the New Lanark community, he was following in the footsteps of David Dale, his father-in-law, who deserved his reputation as one of the most benevolent citizens of Glasgow despite the materialistic motives which he shared with other industrialists of his time. Richard Arkwright, whose improvements upon the water frame made it a practical device, had founded the establishment at New Lanark in 1784 or 1785[1] as a cotton-spinning mill. A partnership formed between Arkwright and Dale had lasted less than two years, whereupon Dale had gained complete control over New Lanark.

Contemporaries credited Dale's factory with the development of the town:

It is to the establishment of this manufacture that we are to deduce the growing prosperity of the latter town. Money is now more frequent there, industry is awakened, and new branches of trade are carried on which had before no existence in the neighbourhood.[2]

Robert Dale Owen, who was Owen's son and Dale's grandson, described Dale as "rich but open-handed, determined, yet tender, sturdily upright but merciful to those who went astray."[3] In an era when most mill owners were concerned only about profits, when workers customarily labored overlong hours under barely tolerable conditions, Dale viewed his proper role as that of paternalistic protector of his employees. The best way to care for his charges, he thought, was to govern New Lanark strictly but with his employees' interests in mind. The community considered him to be a liberal, kindly employer and held him in high esteem.

But Dale was not beyond reproach; in accordance with the practices of the time he permitted the forced labor of children who were

51

taken out of the workhouses in nearby towns and committed to work in his mills. Some five hundred pauper children labored at New Lanark. They were on their feet thirteen hours daily (from 6 A.M. to 7 P.M.), running the machines, susceptible to injuries, fatigue, and disease, common evils afflicting children in all the factories. Dale's mills, however, compared favorably with the other mills, for he saw to it that the children were well clothed, well fed, and well housed in clean, spacious dormitories and received medical attention in time of illness. His contemporaries admired Dale's efforts in behalf of the physical, mental, and moral well-being of the children at New Lanark. They credited him with "a degree of success hitherto unprecedented at any other public works in this kingdom."[4] Yet Dale's benevolence could not combat the evils of the new industrial system.

Dale hoped to teach the children to read and write; he encouraged them to study in the evenings after work. Yet, at the end of the workday they were so exhausted that they could scarcely manage to keep awake, and all attempts to educate them were futile. Dale's intentions were apparently benevolent, but his methods were ineffective, a shortcoming which Owen later attempted to explain in apologetic terms when he wrote that Dale would have preferred to take only older pauper children into his mills, but that he was given no choice in the matter and had to accept those whom the charity institutions sent him. Some of Dale's workers were no more than six or seven years old.

It would have been difficult for Dale to institute drastic reforms efficiently, despite his interest in mill conditions and workers' welfare, for he was an absentee employer who visited the mills only once every three or four months and was unknown to many of his workers. The business was generally left in the care of various employees such as Dale's half brother James Dale and William Kelley, and, instead of following a uniform policy, each departmental manager did whatever he thought was right. As a result, according to Owen, the mill workers, in spite of Dale's beneficence, were plagued with frequent idleness, poverty, excessive debt, a high crime rate, and ill-health, all in all a miserable state of affairs. Furthermore, Dale indulged in favoritism, providing preferential treatment for members of the religious sect of Independents which he headed.

I *Employee Relationships*

Robert Owen, however, had quite different ideas about managing New Lanark. He was keenly aware of the evil conditions in the mills and, through constant efforts to alleviate them to win the trust of the workers, he became a model employer. The improvements he introduced in their behalf set a precedent for other manufacturers, although many of them were reluctant to follow his example because they feared the new practices would reduce profits. Few of them shared Owen's high ideals.

I had to change these evil conditions for good ones, and thus, in the due order of nature, according to its unchanging laws, to supersede the inferior and bad characters, created by inferior and bad conditions, by superior and good characters to be created by superior and good conditions. And this is now the course which for the happiness of all should be universally adopted in practice.[5]

Owen's ideals were actually based upon practical considerations; like the inventors of his day, he was not primarily a theoretician, at least not in the beginning, but rather a concerned businessman searching for practical solutions to the problems which confronted him.

One of the first practices he abandoned was that of importing pauper apprentices. His ideas about the proper role of children in society were quite different from those prevailing in his time. Most people regarded children as miniature adults, whereas Owen considered them to be each a unique personality worthy of respect and consideration. He did not permit anyone under ten years of age to work in his mills, and he urged all young children to remain in school to the age of twelve, even though most employers welcomed the labor of children only six or seven years old. He reduced the workday for children by more than two hours, setting a maximum of 10.5 hours.

Unlike his predecessor Dale, he was not an absentee employer but remained close to the community. He made his residence in or near New Lanark and kept track of as many of his employees as possible, encouraging neighborliness and pride in their village. He saw to it that the streets were paved, the houses kept in good repair (remodeled or enlarged when necessary), and central stores established so that workers could purchase high-quality foods at low prices. His enthusiastic interest in the community inspired them to landscape their houses with decorative gardens and to maintain homes and streets in a clean, orderly condition.

Like other mills, the New Lanark mills had previously been plagued by serious problems of theft, drunkenness, and absenteeism, and Owen took prompt remedial action, reorganizing production, instituting meticulous controls over materials, machines, and stock, and closely supervising the employees. In order to prevent theft, he supplemented the new inventory controls with information addressed to the workers, indicating the way in which financial benefits for them would result from eradication of pilfering and also appealing to them (on the basis of self-interest) for social disapproval of those who violated the moral code. Owen and his managers were generous in their praise of honest work well performed, for they knew that recognition and social approval buttressed a worker's pride in accomplishment and helped to make good work habitual. Drunken quarrels or disorderly conduct met with instant disapproval; participants were subjected to pressure by their peers to avoid such evil habits and disturbances. The managers did their best to settle ordinary quarrels in such a way as to spare the feelings of the parties involved. No religious or other faction was accorded favored treatment. All these policies reflected Owen's conviction that human dignity and the principles of fair play must be preserved to insure order and justice in the community. His policies worked so well that, in thirty years as director of the New Lanark mills, Owen never found it necessary to call upon outside authorities, such as magistrates, for assistance or disciplinary action.

II *The Silent Monitor*

The success of Owen's reforms in mill conditions—the shorter workday, higher wages, and improved living conditions—seemed to prove the validity of his theory that happier employees are more dependable and efficient producers. In our own times the same view has been accepted by many manufacturers whose agreements with labor unions provide for such advantages as frequent breaks, a shorter working week, and decision-making by employees. But Owen's reforms were not the result of collective bargaining with employees; they were paternalistic innovations which he introduced for practical business reasons. Nor did he entirely abandon the idea of controlling and disciplining the workers. In fact, he invented a unique device, the "silent monitor," to facilitate evaluation of their deportment. The device consisted of four blocks, each in a different color, indicating the worker's rating. For example, if the block placed at his work space on a given day were black, that would represent bad conduct, the lowest rating, whereas white would represent excellent behavior and personality traits. Intermediate ratings were blue and yellow.

This disciplinary system, applied to all employees, might seem to us today to be appropriate only for very young people (just as some teachers reward children with stars for good behavior in the classroom), but Owen attributed to it his success in maintaining good order, mutual aid, honesty, and happiness among all age groups.

He never punished a worker for misbehavior: "I merely looked at the person and then at the colour,—but never said a word to one of them by way of blame."[6] Peer pressure could promptly be brought to bear upon any offender, for each monitor was kept on public display in the factory. The worker was not reprimanded or punished for his transgressions, but the knowledge that he was in danger of losing the good opinion of his fellow workers invariably impelled him to mend his ways.

The workers feared the social disapproval of their peers and felt a low rating keenly; Owen said that, without consulting the colored blocks, he could often tell from the disappointed expressions on their faces when they had received a low rating. Employees were given the right to complain about the ratings they received if they found them to be unjust, but, according to Owen, it rarely happened that a person felt he had been misjudged.

He was opposed to penalties of any kind because, he said, punishment must always be "unjust to the individual,"[7] since the latter is never responsible for the real cause of his own objectionable behavior. The parents who reared and miseducated an offender are, in Owen's judgment, the real causes of his antisocial behavior, although even the parents probably should not be held entirely responsible for it inasmuch as their own deficiencies must be attributed to *their* predecessors. Owen believed that, because people are not responsible for their character, ideas, and habits, it would be useless, as well as unjust, to punish anyone, even for criminal acts.

The will of man has no power whatever over his opinions; he must, and ever did, and ever will believe what has been, is, or may be impressed on his mind by his predecessors and the circumstances which surround him. It becomes therefore the essence of irrationality to suppose that any human being, from the creation to this day, could deserve praise or blame, reward or punishment, for the prepossessions of early education.[8]

Owen advocated preventive education instead of ex post facto punishment. Eventually his methods were applied in the classrooms at New Lanark. The consequence of a child's misbehavior was immediate social disapproval of his offensive activities (never condemnation of the child as a person) supplemented by logical explanations so that he would realize that he had done wrong, why it was wrong, why it might cause someone unhappiness, and why, therefore, it would lead ultimately to his own unhappiness. According to Owen, this technique worked equally well with adults and with children. Similar theories concerning punishment have been advocated in our own day by teachers who do not reject or condemn the child but require him to cope with social disapproval or other natural consequences of misbehavior. Modern teachers tend to agree with Owen's assertion that imposed punishment is often "pernicious and injurious to the punisher and punished."[9]

III Reactions to Owen's Innovations

Initially many of his employees distrusted Owen whom they at first regarded as an eccentric Englishman (although he had been born in Wales he had come to Scotland after residing for a while in England) attempting to spread foreign ideas in Scotland. In due time, however, his new approaches and programs won their allegiance by virtue of their apparently just and benevolent motivation. One development that particularly impressed the workers occurred during the American embargo of 1806 whereby President Thomas Jefferson cut off all trade with Europe during a period of fifteen months in retaliation for interference by England and France with American shipping. Both countries were attempting to use America as a pawn following the renewal of their war for supremacy on the Continent. Owen was forced to shut down the mills for four months, but, unlike most other employers, he continued to pay full wages to his idle workers, a decision that helped to win their confidence and esteem. Moreover, he had regularly been buying groceries and clothing, of the highest quality, at wholesale prices and reselling them to New Lanark residents at slightly above cost. By means of such methods and by training the people in habits of self-control and thrift, he enabled them to reduce living expenses about one-fourth and also to make progress "in improved health and superior dress and in the general comfort of their houses."[10]

Owen declared the objective of his experiments at New Lanark to be: "To discover the means by which the condition of the poor and working classes could be ameliorated, and with benefit to their employers."[11] He was interested in benefiting the employers in order to provide a stimulus which would encourage them to improve the conditions under which their employees labored. His overriding principle was prevention; he would substitute good practices for poor ones, reward rather than punish, and demonstrate by example the way to live and work in harmony and happiness. He envisioned communities founded on a system of cooperative labor and sharing of expenses, applied both to agriculture and to industry, with each community housing between five hundred and fifteen hundred people. He worked consistently to achieve the goal of cooperative living throughout the world, a lifelong endeavor which earned for him lasting fame as a pioneer, not only in education but also in future reform movements such as producers' and consumers' cooperatives, trade unionism, and socialism.

Owen was able to operate the New Lanark enterprise at a very good profit, but other mill owners were reluctant to adopt his methods. Over an extended period his various partners could not understand, despite gratifying profits, how his decision to raise wages and shorten hours could be anything other than wasteful and, fearing the possibility of financial losses, they opposed and restricted his program.

His new partners, however, agreed that an employer has a duty to protect the interests of his workers, that he has no right to treat them solely as a means of deriving profit from which they would not benefit. Owen allocated a large share of mill profits to services in behalf of the employees, thereby stimulating their enthusiasm for the work and increasing productivity. He was invariably charitable and considerate to the employees, although directly or indirectly exercising control over their work and life style. He was convinced that workers cannot provide for their own needs without direction or determine their own destiny, that they must be led onto the right paths by beneficent people in the upper classes, men of high birth, ample wealth, and superior intelligence.

Proud of his successful programs at New Lanark, he concluded that they could easily be duplicated everywhere and would eventually improve all social systems and human nature itself.

For twenty-nine years we did without the necessity for magistrates or lawyers; without a single legal punishment; without any known poor's rate; without intemperance or religious animosities. We reduced the hours of labour, well educated all the children from infancy, greatly improved the condition of the adults, diminished their daily hours of labour, paid interest of capital, and cleared upwards of £300,000 of profit.[12]

Although his accomplishments in social reform attracted the favorable attention of influential people around the world, he was never completely satisfied with the results. His experiments had been handicapped by the fact that when he initiated them the community had already established undesirable behavior patterns and practices which were very difficult to modify. He complained, too, that New Lanark, being a one-industry town, could never become entirely self-sufficient.

Robert Dale Owen explained that the experiment could not "be considered as a full and complete, but, on the contrary, as merely a partial and imperfect one; and the results thence obtained, however satisfactory, not as those which a system of training rational and consistent throughout, may be expcted to produce, but only as a proof—an encouraging one, it is presumed—of what may be effected even by a distant approximation to it, under the counteraction of numerous prejudices and retarding causes."[13] From the point of view of Owen's visionary ideals, however, the greatest obstacle, about which he could do little, was the impact of irrational and imperfect social systems outside New Lanark. No matter how nearly perfect the social arrangements within the community might become, the local people would still be affected adversely by the evils of the world beyond its boundaries and jurisdiction. In other words, to be truly effective anywhere, social reforms would have to be made worldwide. A new cooperative humanity could evolve only from universal change.

CHAPTER 5

The New Lanark School System

SINCE Owen believed that character is formed for the individual, not by him, and that from his earliest days the infant receives impressions that become important in the development of his character, he concluded that character education should begin at a very young age. He was convinced that "children can be trained to acquire *any language, sentiments, belief, or any bodily habits and manners, not contrary to human nature.*"[1] Furthermore, he purported to have found no difference between children of upper-class parents and children of the lower orders, and declared that he himself preferred to work with young children of the so-called "worst" families. For Owen, all children held the promise of the future. He reiterated his faith in education, stating that the success of his own ideal communities would depend upon the "manner in which the infants and children shall be trained and educated in these schools."[2] Since the older generation had already been inculcated with erroneous learning, it was essential, he believed, to start anew with the youth of today.

In a poem published many years after his purchase of the New Lanark mills in *The Crisis,* a journal he edited from 1832 to 1834, he expresses his profound faith in early childhood education:

> Train up thy children, England,
> In the ways of righteousness—and feed them
>   With the bread of wholesome doctrine.
> Where hast thou thy mines—but in their industry?
> Thy bulwarks where—but in their breasts? Thy might—
>   But in their arms?
> Must not their numbers, therefore be thy Wealth,
> Thy Strength, thy Power, thy Safety, and thy Pride!
>   Oh! grief, then grief and shame,

> If in this flourishing land there should be dwellings
> Where the new-born babe doth bring unto its parent's soul
> No joy! where squalid Poverty receives it at the birth
> And on her withered knees
> Gives it the scanty bread of discontent.[3]

I *Owen's Plan for New Schools*

Education was the core around which Owen's philosophy centered. Consequently, through the years he had awaited an opportunity to carry out his ambitious plan for a radically new type of school. Now, in New Lanark, he proposed to organize a New Institution for the Formation of Character to include an infant school and an adult school. This new system of education would be the primary means of solving major problems of society. Owen declared that "only by education rightly understood, . . . communities of men can ever be well governed, and by means of such education every object of human society will be attained with the least labour and the most satisfaction."[4]

Education, as Owen interpreted it, governed the mind, the body, and the conscience of the child. Owen's daughter, Jane Dale Owen, defined education as her father intended: "I speak of it [education] now in an extended sense—the only sense in which it ought to be understood—as signifying a general superintendence of the individual from birth to maturity; thus including the cultivation of all his powers, physical, mental, and moral, and the placing him under such circumstances as are best suited for the development of his character."[5]

Education was to be a "moral lever" whereby "ignorance, poverty, disunion, vice, crime, evil passions, and misery"[6] could all be eradicated. Children were to be taught good habits from infancy, to be rationally educated, and to be usefully employed so as to acquire "health of body and peace of mind."[7] The infant school was intended to be "the first practical step towards forming an intelligent, kind, charitable, and rational character for the infants of the human race."[8] The ultimate goal of Owen's system of education at New Lanark was to prepare all young children for "an entirely new state of society—a state based solely on truth, emanating from an accurate practical knowledge of human nature."[9] The name of the school system (New Institution for the Formation of Character) reflected its basic aim: moral improvement through education.

The plan for the New Institution was rejected by Owen's partners on the ground that it would be too costly (it would cost thirty to forty thousand dollars) and would not be immediately productive of income. He had originally bought out several partners in the New Lanark mills because they had opposed his plan to educate the mill workers. He had then formed another partnership, but now the new partners also refused to cooperate in his program, and eventually, despite the fact that Owen owned the largest share of the property, objected to his continuing as manager of the establishment.

Moreover, they refused to sell their shares to him or to buy his interest, but insisted on selling the mills at public auction; next they set about discrediting the worth of New Lanark in the hope of buying it back themselves at a bargain price. Owen, however, had not been idle during this period. In seeking support for his experiment, he wrote, published, and distributed the treatise, *A New View of Society.* Then he traveled to London to find financial backing for his plans. Successful in this quest, he returned to Glasgow in time for the auction and outbid his former partners for the mills.

Owen's new partners, who were as keenly interested as he in his proposed reforms, included John Walker of Arno's Grove, a wealthy, benevolent Quaker (the nickname for members of the Society of Friends founded by George Fox in 1647); John Foster of Bromley, also a Quaker; William Allen of Plough Court, a leader in the Society of Friends, who became the most active and ambitious of the new partners; Jeremy Bentham, the noted jurist and social reformer, undoubtedly the best known of the partners; Joseph Fox, a dentist, who was a dissenter from the Church of England: and Michael Gibbs (a relative of Fox) who later became an alderman and the Lord Mayor of London. Owen owned five of the thirteen shares in the partnership. The partners trusted Owen, and some of them never came to visit the establishment which they all helped to support. Since all of them depended upon him to cope with policies and administrative problems, he was at last enabled to put his cherished plan into operation. From several partners and others, however, he encountered skeptical reactions to his unprecedented proposals. "I had then . . . to overcome the prejudices of the parents against sending their children so young to school. I had to meet the objections of my partners, who were all good commercial men, and looked to the main chance, as they termed it,—which was a good return for their capital."[10]

Besides reassuring his partners, he succeeded in convincing the parents that taking their very young children out of the home would be justified by the benefits to be derived from the school program. He also persuaded many of the parents to participate in night classes and attend lectures at the New Institution.

Owen foresaw little difficulty in teaching parents what "is right and proper,"[11] anticipating that the only problem would be "to unlearn those pernicious habits and sentiments"[12] that had been handed down from one generation to the next. In his plan for the New Institution, facilities were to be made available evenings to older children and adults for reading, writing, mathematics, sewing, conversation, dancing, and music. Participating adults ideally would come to understand the beneficial results of such a rational type of education for their children, become enthusiastic sponsors, and at the same time acquire greater skill in coping with family problems and responsibilities. Owen promised the adults under his supervision that they would "acquire superior habits; your minds will gradually expand."[13]

II   *The New Institution for the Formation of Character*

The two-story building for the new schools (organized in 1816) had five rooms and housed as many as six hundred children. The two rooms in the upper story, equipped with double rows of windows, were spacious enough to accommodate large audiences. The main room was furnished on the Lancasterian model: desks were separated by a center aisle, a pulpit at one end, and galleries for visitors adjacent to the other three sides. This main room was used for lectures and religious services. (No attempt was made to follow the Lancasterian method of teaching whereby hundreds of pupils studied academic subjects in a single room with older pupils serving as assistant teachers.) The other room was used for lectures, dancing, and singing. On its walls were numerous animal and mineral specimens, for Owen believed strongly in visual aids. Maps of various countries and bodies of water were displayed at one end of the room, but without labels inasmuch as the children were required to insert the names, an activity regarded as more beneficial than the mere memorization of such information.

The first floor of the building contained three smaller rooms, each twelve feet high. Owen planned the rooms with the needs of the children in mind. English buildings were not centrally heated at that time. Owen had hollow iron pillars installed to serve as heat conductors so that throughout the year the building could be kept at a comfortable temperature. The downstairs rooms were used for reading, natural history, and geography. The pupils participated in small-group activities, the size of the classes usually ranging from twenty to forty children. Those under seven years of age were taught together; older boys and girls were taught separately and met only for singing, dancing, and lectures. Pupils eight to ten years old devoted two hours daily to dancing and music.

One teacher was assigned to each class. The staff included, in addition to teachers of academic subjects, a number of specialists who taught singing, dancing, sewing, and military drill. The pupils attended class about 5½ hours, beginning at 7:30 A.M., except for those under five years of age who spent half of their school time in unstructured play. All children enjoyed spontaneous play during recesses between classes.

For the year 1816, as shown in the following chart, Owen reported a total attendance of 444 children, ranging in age from three to ten years, evidence that his experiment had begun on a fairly large scale.

Males	Females	Total	Ages (Yrs.)
35	25	60	3
27	19	46	4
29	30	59	5
27	21	48	6
34	22	56	7
26	24	50	8
30	23	53	9
38	34	72	10
246	198	444	3-10, inclusive[14]

III   *The Infant School*

Robert Dale Owen wrote that "The system of education which has been introduced at New Lanark differs essentially from any that has been adopted in a similar institute in the United Kingdom, or, probably in any other part of the world."[15] One of the major educational innovations at New Lanark, and perhaps the one afforded most visibility, was the Infant School.

The Lutheran pastor Jean Frédéric Oberlin had organized an infant school in France in 1769, paving the way for the famous French "mother schools" (*écoles maternelles*), but Owen developed his program independently. Children were admitted to the Infant School as soon as they were able to walk. Usually from thirty to fifty pupils ranging in age from one to three years, attended this school, which became a model for modern nursing schools. The purpose of the Infant School was twofold: to save these very young children from the harmful influence of their parents and to teach them good habits. Owen asserted that "in ninety-nine cases out of a hundred, parents are altogether ignorant of the right method of treating children, and their own children especially."[16] Character education could not be left to parents but must be provided for infants by trained personnel: "To form the most superior character for the human race, the training and education should commence from the birth of the child; and to form a good character they must begin systematically when the child is one year old. But much has been done rightly or wrongly before that period. From that age on no child should be brought up isolated."[17]

Owen was convinced that good habits begun in infancy would remain throughout the individual's life. He hoped to inculcate habits of good health in the infants. His program for nurturing young children included:

1st.   Kind treatment, with judgment, from birth.
2nd.   Pure air.
3rd.   Wholesome food in proper quantity, and at proper times.
4th.   Regular exercise in the open air through life.
5th.   Due cultivation of all the faculties, powers, and qualities, physical and mental.
6th.   The temperate exercise of all the natural propensities, at their proper periods through life.

7th.   Healthy alternate occupation of body and mind; temperate in
        proportion to the strength and capacity of the individual.

8th.   Extensive real knowledge of ourselves, society, and nature, in accor-
        dance with facts and external nature, without mysteries to confound
        the understanding and judgment, or any of the other faculties of the
        mind.

9th.   Full, genuine, and pure charity, derived from an accurate
        knowledge of human nature, which produces kindness for all, and
        destroys all the inferior passions and all motives to vice and crime;
        generating a serenity of mind and feeling, self-possession, and
        satisfaction, from which alone a constant good state of physical and
        mental health can proceed. And

10th.   The esteem and affection of all our neighbours and friends, and of
        the human race. [18]

Great care was exercised in the selection of teachers for children
in the Infant School. Only women teachers who loved children and
also knew how to impart information to them were acceptable,
teachers capable of winning the children's confidence and establishing a climate of mutual respect and affection. Every teacher
was expected to treat pupils with sympathy and kindness (without
spoiling them as was too often done by their mothers) and to answer
their questions much better than the parents could.

The program included answering children's questions (for example, through informal conversation and nature study) and moral and
physical training. Pictures, models, and maps were used, as well as
nature objects and games, but no books. The children often
preferred to play outdoors and were allowed to do so when weather
permitted instead of participating in classroom lessons. They were
allowed to schedule activities and rest periods for themselves. At
any one time, several different activities might be in progress, for
there was no uniform, imposed activity program for all. "Useless
childish toys" [19] were rejected; companionship and cooperative
group projects were encouraged.

Kindness and sympathy pervaded the atmosphere of the Infant
School. Owen seemed to feel that female teachers would be more
capable of responding to the children's needs with patience and
affection than would their male counterparts, but he urged that all
teachers should be trained adequately in order to establish the best
rapport with their pupils. As in our own modern schools, there was a

high degree of self-direction and permissiveness for children in the Infant School, and this policy required skillful, tactful guidance by well-trained teachers.

The principle around which the Infant School revolved was that infants must be prevented from receiving erroneous information and forming undesirable habits.

Our duty then is to guard against his [the infant's] receiving any other than *right* ideas; and in order to effect this, our own actions must be regulated. He ought never to be made the recipient of anger, nor be witness to it; the tone of voice ever expressing to him feelings of the utmost kindness. He ought, as an infant, to be presented with no objects but those which it may be beneficial for him to examine; as his natural curiosity prompting him so to do, he is often, upon refusal led into ebullitions of passion, which gradually become habitual. He should have no deceit practised upon him, nor made a participator by any. Thus guarding, in the earliest period of his existence, against every contingency which may communicate to him evil habits, we shall, when he has attained sufficient age, have a fair field upon which to enter, in the cultivation of his moral qualities.[20]

Since Owen believed that the character traits developed by very young children persist in their maturity and thereby determine the attitudes and habits of the adult community, he gave the highest priority to the program of the Infant School. He wrote that "men are, and ever will be, what they are and shall be made in infancy and childhood."[21] He fondly hoped that education beginning in infancy would become effective enough to produce a generation of morally superior human beings. Man has learned how to raise a more desirable breed of animals and certainly should be able to obtain comparable results in the rearing of children. In fact, said Owen, children will eventually be trained so skillfully that they will develop any traits desired by the community provided that such traits are "not contrary to human nature."[22] A hundred years later, Sigmund Freud arrived at the same conclusion as Owen concerning the decisive importance of early childhood experiences and agreed that adults could readily guide infants to form desired habits but would find it much more difficult to help older children to unlearn bad habits. Owen's views on this subject are currently finding acceptance among intelligent parents, trained teachers, and educational psychologists.

IV   *The Playground*

Owen's conviction that children cannot learn properly, develop good habits, or derive sufficient emotional satisfaction and self-expression in their homes impelled him to provide his pupils with opportunities for enjoyable games, exercises, and morally uplifting experiences on the school playground. He knew that play activities of children are not merely sources of entertainment or relaxation, as comparable activities of adults often are, but methods of enriching their intellectual lives, a serious yet happy means of self-expression, learning, and mutual understanding. The golden rule of the New Lanark playground admonished every child to strive to make all his companions successful and happy. The same ideal has motivated play activities in modern nursery schools and kindergartens in which the moral, social, and emotional growth of each child is the dominant aim.

Present-day psychologists agree with Owen's statement concerning the necessity of providing for the emotional needs of young children: "If adults would patiently encourage them to express candidly what they thought and felt, much suffering would be saved to the children."[23] He felt certain that as soon as older children had been taught habits of candid self-expression and mutual aid, they would set an example for younger ones to emulate so that repressed feelings, deviousness, and other "pernicious sentiments" would no longer prevent satisfactory emotional adjustment, learning, and character education. (This idea that, if properly trained, some children will guide others by example was not a new departure; it was the principal feature in the contemporary monitorial schools of Joseph Lancaster and Andrew Bell, in which older pupils instructed younger ones in skills which they themselves had already mastered.)

Owen felt confident that the happiness ensuing from the practice of cooperation in play activities would induce all pupils to observe this approved mode of conduct until it became a natural, enduring characteristic of their behavior. Such conduct would become second nature to the child, who would then be worthy of being respected as a "rational" person.

In playground activities, as in other school programs, due consideration was given to the interests and needs of the participants, even with regard to such details as the choice of costumes. (The children wore white cotton Roman-style tunics, knee-length for boys and ankle-length for girls, which contributed to their comfort and ease of movement.) In his discussion of desirable educational reforms prior to the opening of the New Institution, Owen had pointed out the advantages of playground activities. For a large part of the day children would be cared for by trained teachers well qualified for the task instead of being miseducated by untrained parents unfit for such responsibilities. The parents would then have more time to further their own education and personal interests. The identical advantages have recently been cited by modern proponents of women's rights; and mothers today who wish to pursue their education or careers welcome the organization of child care centers in which their children can find safety and obtain proper guidance and stimulating experiences like those provided on the New Lanark playground. The following statement of advantages would be appreciated by adherents of child care centers: "The child will be placed in a situation of safety, where, with its future school-fellows and companions, it will acquire the best habits and principles, while at meal times and at night it will return to the caresses of its parents; and the affections of each are likely to be increased by the separation."[24]

Owen indicated that the use of the playground would not be restricted to younger pupils, that all the children would benefit from the accessibility of the large playground: "The area is also to be a place of meeting for the children from five to ten years of age, previous to and after school-hours, and to serve for a drill ground, the object of which will be hereafter explained; and a shade will be formed, under which in stormy weather the children may retire for shelter."[25]

Owen explained that the purpose of drill exercises, which were to be directed by a retired soldier, would be to prepare boys for military service in defense of the country. Although he was a pacifist and believed that character education would remake human nature so that all peoples would live in peace, this process would, he thought, take time and in the interim citizens should be equipped to defend the nation against any aggressor. Moreover, the drill exercises would develop the boys' physical strength and skill and teach them the values of order, obedience, and discipline. On the other hand, the pupils would be taught to use only as much force as

necessary for protection against their enemies. He advocated training of boys for service in an army of reserves ready for action in war
emergencies, a program limited in scope so as not to interfere with
their productivity as workers and their functions as cooperative
citizens in peacetime.

V   *The Program of Instruction*

Owen had faith in the capacity of children to take an active, self-
directive part in the learning process. Pupils at New Lanark were
permitted to initiate many activities based upon their own felt interests. He urged teachers to provide intellectually stimulating objects in the classroom (such as pictures and charts, as well as plants
and other objects found in nature) and to adapt instruction to the
children's natural curiosity about the materials on display. Pupils
were asked to identify objects, both animate and inanimate, and to
enlarge their knowledge about them by proceeding always from the
known to the unknown. This teaching method was devised by
Owen so that the children would become acquainted with objects in
nature directly before attempting to acquire additional information
through artificial symbols such as descriptive statements or verbal
abstractions.

Our modern schools apply the same principle of teaching when
they organize excursions to zoos, farms, fire stations, museums, and
the like to prepare children for reading assignments. The pupils at
New Lanark took nature walks near their school and collected or
made notes about interesting objects, often asking questions which
their teacher answered informally; later, they discussed in the
classroom relevant pictures, charts, and written symbols or gener-
alizations. Although class discussions were not structured in advance, they most often moved from the specific to the general. It
was Owen's view that the most significant task in the imparting of
knowledge is to sustain the pupils' interest at a peak level of intensity.

The principle of learning from concrete objects to abstract conclusions was not restricted to nature study. In the study of human
relationships, for example, teachers were trained to explain the
structure of society by displaying a pyramid of wooden blocks
representing the social classes of Great Britain at that time, a type of

visual aid which Owen hoped would stimulate "an animated conversation between the children and their instructors, now themselves acquiring new knowledge by attempting to instruct their
young friends, as I always taught them to think their pupils were,
and to treat them as such."[26] The child's life experience with
natural and social phenomena would precede his attempt to learn
from books. The teachers at New Lanark were to follow nature's
lead in guiding children onto the paths of knowledge and truth.
Owen wrote:

With regard to the instruction to be given at the schools, it is proposed that
the mode of communicating knowledge by means of sensible signs and of
conversations with the teacher, shall supersede, for a considerable period,
the usual practice of learning from books, which, if commenced before the
child can have acquired an adequate number of correct and useful ideas, is
calculated, not only to disgust him, but to fill his head with mere words, to
which either no ideas or very erroneous ideas are attached, and thus
materially to injure his faculties and retard or prevent his intellectual improvement.
    In short, in this case, as well as in every other, we must follow, not
counteract nature.[27]

Owen believed that "the strength and capacity"[28] of the minds of
children had never been correctly tested because they had until
then been judged only on the basis of the limited and faulty instruction given to them. Consequently, he said, man's maximal capacity
for learning and the full extent of his intelligence remained unknown.
    Girls and boys participated equally in school activities, with the
exceptions of military drill, which was restricted to boys, and some
special classes in homemaking designed for girls. Although in the
early nineteenth century equal education for both sexes was considered unusual and unnecessary, Owen insisted that girls should be
afforded every possible opportunity for self-education and community service which might arise. He expected girls to become not
only competent homemakers, but also skilled workers contributing
their full share to the economic welfare of society, all the more so
since the social arrangements he advocated would require less time
than formerly for rearing children. He included, in addition to

regular subjects, special classes exclusively for girls, to teach them sewing, the preparation of meals, and housekeeping—skills previously neglected in New Lanark.

In general, however, school activities were shared experiences of girls and boys, each eager to enhance the successes and happiness of all the others. The practice of cooperation and mutual aid united the children and became a part of their lifelong motivation as they studied and played together "as though they were literally all of one family."[29] The care and education of children by trained personnel in such an ideal setting and cooperative atmosphere has been attempted in a few modern communities, such as the cooperative settlements of Israel (the *kibbutzim*). Owen predicted that this type of educational experience would create a new generation of human beings endowed with compassion, mutual respect, and integrity, and would elevate the community to unprecedented heights of morality and happiness.

CHAPTER 6

Teachers at New Lanark

O WEN realized that teachers for the New Lanark schools would have to be selected with utmost care because they would be expected to assume great responsibilities requiring high character and an inspiring personality rather than intellectual powers or attainments. It was imperative, he thought, for teachers to win the admiration, trust, and friendship of their pupils. His teachers were expected to convey a message of kindness in tone, word, look, and action to all children at all times and in this way win their confidence. They were never to show, hopefully never feel, preference for one child over another.

I *Qualifications of Teachers*

Flexibility in classroom activities was a fundamental requirement, and no hard and fast schedules were to be observed. Owen decided that young teachers would be more likely than older ones to fit into his school programs, which necessitated quick adjustments to rapidly changing situations. Children would always receive courteous, rational answers to their questions. Teachers would be frank, honest, and fair in their relationships to pupils. If teachers could not answer children's questions at times, they would admit their lack of knowledge, never attempting to evade an issue or supply possibly erroneous information. *"Each individual is so organized that he must necessarily become irrational, when he is made from infancy to receive as truths false notions; and can only become rational, when he shall be made from infancy to receive true ideas without any admixture to error."*[1]

New Lanark teachers would have to be nature lovers, enthusiastic about outdoor life, because children might at any time decide to shift their activities to out-of-school locations, changing their plans in accordance with weather conditions and their own interests.

Owen advocated special programs for the preparation of teachers. All teachers would have to become trained professionals. He selected his staff on the basis of their personality traits and then taught them his pedagogical methods. Assuming that new teachers could never instruct children properly if they themselves had been imperfectly educated, he proposed that schools for prospective teachers be organized throughout Great Britain. He declared that, unless teachers had been educated so that they acquired adequate knowledge and conducted themselves as rational persons should, the whole educational enterprise would be sabotaged by the very act of defective teaching.

At present there are not any individuals in the kingdom [Great Britain] who have been trained to instruct the rising generation as it is for the interest and happiness of all that it should be instructed. The training of those who are to form the future man, becomes a consideration of the utmost magnitude; for, on due reflection, it will appear, that instruction to the young must be, of necessity, the only foundation upon which the superstructure of society can be raised. Let this instruction continue to be left, as heretofore, to chance, and often to the most inefficient members of the community, and society must still experience the endless miseries which still arise from such weak and puerile conduct. On the contrary, let the instruction to the young be well-devised and well-executed, and no subsequent proceedings in the state can be materially injurious.[2]

In the selection of teachers, character traits of kindness and patience were particularly emphasized because the staff would never be permitted to scold children or punish them for misbehavior. Such discipline was regarded as unjust and futile inasmuch as, in Owen's opinion, misbehavior is always the result of miseducation of children. Furthermore, the administering of rewards and punishments could lead to the perpetuation of just such characteristics, as pride and vanity, or hopelessness and despair, as Owen wished to eradicate in future generations. Rewards and punishments were said by Robert Dale Owen to be,

"Unjust—as, on the one hand loading those individuals with supposed advantages and distinctions, whom Providence, either in the formation of their talents and dispositions, or in the character of their parents and associates, seems already to have favoured; and on the other, as inflicting farther pain on those, whom less fortunate, or less favourable circumstances, have already formed into weak, vicious, or ignorant,—or in other words, into unhappy beings.

And prejudicial—in rendering a strong, bold character, either proud and overbearing, or vindictive and deceitful; or in instilling into the young mind, if more timid and less decided, either an overweening opinion of its own abilities and endowments, or a dispiriting idea of its own incompetency—such an idea as creates a sullen, hopeless despondency, and destroys that elasticity of spirit, from whence many of our best actions proceed, but which is lost as soon as the individual feels himself sunk, mentally or morally, below his companions, disgraced by punishment, and treated with neglect or contempt by those around him."[3]

Reward, Robert Dale Owen warned, could conceivably lead to displays of "pride, vanity, and inordinate ambition,"[4] whereas punishment could be responsible for "debasing the character, and destroying the energies of the individual."[5]

Owen announced that "every child . . . will always be treated kindly, whatever his natural character, physical or mental, may be."[6]

He insisted that all teachers appointed to the New Lanark schools accept and implement his view concerning discipline that so-called "bad" individuals, those who transgress the rules of society, do so only because their parents and community have miseducated them and therefore should be accorded sympathy, not anger or hostility. Teachers at New Lanark would have to be tolerant persons with positive attitudes toward children, perhaps at times expressing approval or disapproval but never resorting to rewards or punishments. When correction of inappropriate behavior was necessary, it was to be given "in the spirit of kindness and of charity, as from the more experienced, to the less experienced,"[7] and was never to arouse feelings of guilt or inadequacy in the child. Owen explained the rationale for this new departure in school discipline:

The infants and children of every generation have been the mental slaves of the preceding generations. . . . they have been compelled to become—what their fathers had been previously compelled to be—slaves to the most gross and inconsistent errors, which rendered them to all intents and purposes, much more irrational in their thoughts, feelings, and actions, than any other species of animals, yet claimants to a superiority of intellect over the unerring instincts of the latter.[8]

Owen predicted that well-qualified teachers would not only relieve misbehaving children of the fear and burden of futile punishment but also set an example of compassion, understanding, and ethical conduct for them to emulate, and thus counteract the results of undesirable home environments.

II *James Buchanan and Molly Young*

When he selected his first teachers for the New Lanark schools, Owen gave preference to applicants without previous professional training or experience. Untrained teachers would, he believed, serve the needs of the children better than experienced teachers who had been instructed in the wrong attitudes and methods of the old system of education. He wanted teachers who had a "great love for and unlimited patience with infants."[9] Above all else, he sought the very best teachers for the infant school because he knew that "if the foundation were not truly laid, it would be in vain to expect a satisfactory structure."[10]

He chose James Buchanan, a weaver and lay preacher from Edinburgh, to be the first headmaster of the New Institution for the Formation of Character. Buchanan, according to Owen, was a simple-minded individual scarcely able to read and write, who impressed him as an outgoing, warm-hearted person who loved children and seemed receptive to training by Owen for his new responsibilities. Owen discovered soon enough that training Buchanan was no quick or easy task, but he persevered and achieved satisfactory results despite interference by the headmaster's wife to whose wishes the headmaster (Buchanan) meekly submitted. Owen commented on the difficulty of training the "docile" Buchanan: "For weeks and months it was necessary for me to be daily present, in order to instruct him in the manual part of that which I wished him to do; and, above all, to infuse into him the true spirit of the system, and the proper method of treating the children. As he was very illiterate, and had everything to learn, it was not easy to teach him how to conduct the infant department."[11]

Owen hired Molly Young, a seventeen-year-old worker in the cotton mills to serve as assistant to the headmaster. She was apparently an intelligent person, possibly better qualified than Buchanan for the top administrative position, but, being a woman and therefore expected to work mainly with the youngest children, had to be content with the subordinate post. As the school programs developed and the number of pupils increased, additional personnel were needed. In 1816 Owen reported to a parliamentary committee on education that he employed one headmaster and ten assistants in the day school. The staff also included three teachers to teach night classes for older children and adults. Owen opposed the practice of organizing large classes which he regarded as a "defect in the present system; it is impossible, in my opinion, for one master to do justice to children, when they attempt to educate a great number without proper assistance."[12]

The headmaster and his assistant received from Owen a long list of rules which he had formulated as a guide or manual to make certain that the methods of instruction utilized would implement his educational philosophy, with special emphasis upon two principles: (1) there would be no punishment of children for misbehavior; (2) every effort would be made to insure spontaneity, mutual aid, and happiness among children during the learning process.

The first instruction which I gave them [Buchanan and Young] was, that they were on no account ever to beat any one of the children, or to threaten them in any manner in word or action, or to use abusive terms; but were always to speak to them with a pleasant countenance, and in a kind manner and tone of voice. That they should tell the infants and children (for they had all from one to six years old under their charge) that they must on all occasions do all they could to make their playfellows happy,—and that the older ones, from four to six years of age, should take especial care of younger ones, and should assist to teach them to make each other happy.

The children were not to be annoyed with books; but were to be taught the uses and nature or qualities of the common things around them, by familiar conversation when the children's curiosity was excited so as to induce them to ask questions respecting them.[13]

As a result of Owen's philosophy, the teachers at New Lanark were loved and not feared; pupils felt free to approach the teachers out of school; the behavior of the class did not deteriorate when the teachers' backs were turned. The atmosphere of respect and mutual trust thus engendered encouraged the children to pursue their educational interests without fear of criticism or ridicule.

Under Owen's direction, Buchanan and the staff combined the teaching of conventional subjects, such as nature study and history, with instruction in ethical conduct, morality, and cooperative human relationships. Children were taught high ideals in accordance with Owen's philosophy of life which emphasized the necessity for rational, socially useful contributions by every person to the success and happiness of all others in the community. The primary objective of the New Lanark system of education was to implant in the minds of the pupils a logical way of thinking about their mutual needs and responsibilities. Owen felt that his pedagogical methods would reform not only the New Lanark community but would spread far and wide to remake human nature everywhere, and he therefore accepted pupils from neighboring villages who applied for admission to the New Institution.

Buchanan proved himself to be an effective aide to Owen at New Lanark, becoming well known as a headmaster, but eventually resigned to accept a position as manager of an infant school organized in 1819 by a group of civic leaders including the noted jurist, educator, and statesman Lord Henry Peter Brougham and the great Scottish philosopher and economist James Mill. The school in London was not well administered, however, and Owen reported that during a visit to that school he was shocked to see the children cringing in terror while Buchanan's wife threatened to whip them for misbehavior. Owen commented that "as soon as he [Buchanan] was left to his own guidance, he was quite unequal to the organization and management of a school,"[14] and he condemned Buchanan's establishment as "a disgrace to the Infant-School system."[15] Nevertheless, Buchanan remained there almost twenty years, and the London school, perhaps owing largely to its distinguished sponsors, helped to popularize the idea of infant school education in England.

Despite Owen's criticism, there were some who believed Buchanan was a highly innovative teacher who was in great measure responsible for the system of education at New Lanark. Citing Owen's frequent absences from New Lanark to promote his views and to agitate for new factory legislation, Buchanan's supporters said that the teacher himself had devised exercises, lessons, songs, and stories to meet the children's needs. Buchanan's granddaughter, in writings about her grandfather, asserted that he had developed the methods of teaching used at New Lanark and that his wife was not cruel or vindictive but actually practical, shrewd, and competent, the backbone of the school in London. In 1847 *The Westminster and Foreign Quarterly Review* credited Buchanan with the success of the New Lanark program:

James Buchanan succeeded in a task under which all commonplace schoolmasters, wedded to old methods, would have broken down. He found out the art of winning infantile attention,—amused while he instructed his little classes with pictures and objects, instead of books, and made them happy. His success was complete, and the New Lanark children, in great part at least, through his exertions, became an object of attraction to tourists. . . . there is a quiet order of merit which wins our respect by not obtruding itself; a quality in those who are only seen by the public when pushed forward by others, and it is one which always belongs to James Buchanan.[16]

This report describes the experiment at New Lanark correctly even though it credits the wrong person with its success, for Buchanan had merely implemented the plans formulated by Owen. The editors of *The Westminster and Foreign Quarterly Review* knew Buchanan was not an educational theorist but nonetheless felt justified in calling him the "original *founder*" of Infant Schools in Britain because "it is not so much those who with philanthropic objects establish a school, as he who first introduces the plan which makes a school succeed, to whom the country is chiefly indebted for the gift of education."[17]

The New Lanark schools attracted visitors from many parts of the world eager to observe Owen's revolutionary system of education. Owen commented that the schools flourished particularly after Buchanan's departure, but he would probably have been among the first to concede that the former headmaster had carried out instructions effectively and, especially in the early stages, had contributed much to the New Institution. Owen, however, had been the innovator and Buchanan merely his agent, albeit an honest one who never attempted to claim credit for the idea and development of the unprecedented infant schools.[18] Owen's treatises, written before, during, and after the experiment at New Lanark, prove that he had formulated plans for such schools and their novel methods of instruction long before Buchanan came upon the scene.

Owen did not regret Buchanan's departure. Immediately he set about training a new headmaster, this time an alumnus of the New Lanark schools who, though only sixteen years old, was "the best instructor of infants I have ever seen in any part of the new world,"[19] and "had imbibed the true spirit of the system."[20] The new choice "was . . . much in advance of his former master [Buchanan] as a scholar and in habits, became greatly his superior, and by his youth and vigour, aided by a fine enthusiasm in the cause, which I had been enabled to create in him, a rapid advance and improvement were made in the first year after James Buchanan had left the school."[21]

CHAPTER 7

Educational Pioneering at New Lanark

T HE New Lanark schools implemented Owen's principal innovative views concerning proper methods of education. His innovations ranged over a wide area, including the social aims of education, a new approach to the curriculum and teaching methods, religious education, and adult education.

I *Social Aims of Education*

Owen envisaged a perfect society or ideal community divided into the following eight "classes" or groups based primarily on chronological age: (1) infants from birth to the age of five, provided with adequate food, clothing, physical training, and affectionate care; (2) children of five to ten years, educated through conversation and examination of environmental objects so that they would become straight-thinking, rational human beings learning (within the limits of their capacity) about life and the mysterious forces of nature; (3) children ten to fifteen years old trained to perform the principal tasks essential for life in any community, such as gardening, carpentry, and other common activities of citizens; (4) a select group fifteen to twenty years old (already properly educated since birth) specially trained to become leaders of the community, constituting a superior race of people; (5) persons twenty to twenty-five years old serving as instructors of younger children and as producers of food, clothing, and all other goods necessary for the maintenance of the community; (6) persons twenty-five to thirty years of age trained to care for and safeguard the wealth and abundant materials produced by the younger classes; (7) persons of thirty to forty years trained to maintain households and families in harmony with precepts of law and order, cooperation, and mutual aid; (8) persons forty to sixty years of age responsible for the conduct of foreign affairs requiring complicated communication and dealings with outside communities. Persons over sixty years would be free of all responsibility for work or other tasks in the community. Owen predicted that his ideal society of eight classes (contrasted with Plato's ideal society of only three classes, namely guardians, soldiers, and workers) would be achieved by applying his system of education for children and reeducation for adults, and that it would thereafter be self-perpetuating as a perfect world community.

All eight classes would have their respective roles and functions in society, none being regarded as inferior or superior to the others. To prepare children for life in this egalitarian ideal society, said Owen, a uniform system of education would be necessary whereby every child would receive the best training and education that could be made available to him, without regard to his particular social class or the accident of birth into a particular family or group. Owen explained this point of view in an editorial published in *The Crisis:*

If we are asked "What sort of education is good enough for the common people?" we ask in reply, "What sort of education is good enough for the richest and most favored classes in the land?" The answer to the one question, is, with us, the answer to the other.

We do not enquire then, "what is good enough for the common people?" we enquire "what is good enough for human beings?" What makes a man better, wiser, a more enlightened citizen, a more useful member of society? If we are asked whether we propose arithmetic, astronomy, history, the modern languages, chemistry, physiology, comparative anatomy, drawing, music, as branches which should be taught to every child in the republic; we reply, if any one, or if several, or if all the branches are essentially useful to human beings—if they contribute to mental cultivation, to moral improvement, and if they do not occupy time which might be more importantly employed—we do most assuredly propose them as proper to be taught in all state schools, to every child, rich or poor, patrician or plebeian. We may chance to consider some branches of study which now occupy much time, unfit for public schools. But, if we do, it will be, not because they are too good for the people, but too useless for them; not because they are fit only for the rich, but because they are fit for nobody.

When we propose a system of republican education for the people, therefore, we propose that it should be *the best*—not the most brilliant, not the most extravagantly expensive, not the most fashionable—but *the best* that the nation in its wisdom, may be able to devise.[1]

The program of education at New Lanark was designed to achieve practical objectives; it was planned as a pragmatic, utilitarian means of equipping each child with the knowledge, skills, and character whereby he would fulfill a useful role in the community. Owen's teaching methods were applied to both academic and technical-vocational subjects. In his view all children could master mechanical skills as easily, and in the same way, as they learned reading, writing, and arithmetic. The best possible education in diversified subjects and skills, together with moral development and character training, was needed as much by the children of affluent parents as by those living in poverty. To make it clear to all citizens that his system of education was designed not for the poor only, but for all children, Owen charged the parents a nominal fee of three pennies per month for each child in attendance. The parents willingly paid the fee. The cost of the program per child was two pounds annually,[2] but he was glad to make up the financial deficit in return for "the improved character of the whole population, upon whom the school had a powerful influence for good."[3]

II *The Teaching of School Subjects*[4]

The curriculum at New Lanark centered around subject matter and skills that could be put to practical use in life situations; Owen rejected the traditional emphasis upon learning for its own sake or learning as a means of mental discipline. He opposed the prevailing method of teaching which depended upon drill and memorization of "precept upon precept, and line upon line."[5] His philosophy of education required an emphasis upon practical applications and clear understanding of subject matter. That emphasis, he insisted, should be applied both to academic studies and to skills such as carpentry and gardening. Learning activities, he said, must be practical, brief, spontaneous, enjoyable, and recreational.

He listed the basic subjects, knowledge, skills, and attitudes, as follows:

Reading, writing and accounts.

The elements of the most useful sciences, including mechanics and chemistry.

A practical knowledge of agriculture and domestic economy, with a knowledge of some one useful manufacture, trade, or occupation, so that his employment may be varied, for the improvement of his mental and physical powers.

And, lastly, a knowledge of himself and of human nature, to form him into a rational being, and render him charitable, kind, and benevolent to all his fellow-creatures.[6]

The curriculum included not only the three Rs and vocational training, but also nature study, geography, history, principles of Christianity, music, and dancing. It was a utilitarian amalgam of basic skills, practical knowledge, civic and aesthetic studies, and ethical principles.

The latter received special attention; even during infancy, children were trained in habits of moral conduct so that they would always give priority to the happiness of their companions above all other considerations. Older groups received training again to reinforce ethical values in their everyday behavior. At the same time, on all age levels the basic skills and formal subjects of the curriculum were not slighted nor neglected.

Owen believed that children must be taught to read well and in such a way that they will clearly understand everything they read. Therefore, he did not accede to the parents' requests that their children be taught to read at an early age. He warned against mistaking the means for the end, reminding adults that reading was just a tool through which knowledge could be transmitted. The early mastering of reading skills was not to be attempted at the sacrifice of comprehension or satisfaction.

Owen was far ahead of his time in regard to methodology. Although he did not have the benefit of psychological researches, he had been a keen observer of children's behavior and had concluded that life experiences should be the foundation of reading materials and instruction. Consequently he did not attempt to teach reading to pupils at New Lanark before the age of seven or eight. For younger children, he included preparations for reading that were remarkably similar to modern reading-readiness programs, making use of informal talks, pictures, stories, and outings as means of familiarizing the children with objects and natural phenomena in the immediate environment. His reading-readiness program was designed to broaden children's interests and stimulate their desire to expand upon their store of knowledge by learning to read and thus to explore a new world of meaningful information. But Owen was cautious about the selection and use of books. He excluded books entirely from the curriculum for children under six years of age since there were too few such materials geared to their special needs and he characterized most of the sophisticated writings then available as "generally worse than useless,"[7] beyond the comprehension of the young readers—even though he himself during childhood had read a great deal of adult-oriented literature, including histories, biographies, and novels. Only a few books were accepted as suitable for pupils under ten years of age. Owen gave preference to anecdotal books of travel containing illustrations and maps, and he also approved of popular novels for children and adults by Maria Edgeworth. Books were studied in the classroom in an economical and efficient manner. Only one copy of a book was used, and either a pupil or the teacher would read from it orally, using intonations such as those normally used in conversation to show the meaning of the passage. The children listened attentively so that they would be ready to answer questions about the material.

Handwriting was regarded as another important practical subject in the New Lanark curriculum. Owen felt that children should learn to write "expeditiously a good legible hand,"[8] and the teaching method he advocated required the pupils to master a legible "business" type of handwriting as opposed to a formal, stiff school script by a procedure still used in many of our modern schools. The handwriting models prepared by the teacher dealt with various school subjects such as history and geography. The children would demonstrate their ability to copy the teacher's specimens correctly and would then write and memorize verbatim important information dictated to them.

A similarly practical approach was applied to the teaching of arithmetic. Pupils learned the basic mathematical rules and applications of those rules, but they did not merely commit them to memory. They were taught the relationships and meanings involved in arithmetical calculations so that they gained an understanding of them and could apply the knowledge and skill thus acquired to real life situations.

The lecture, recitation, and question-answer methods were used in teaching natural history, geography, and history to classes consisting of forty to fifty pupils.

The subject matter studied in natural history classes dealt mainly with biological facts relating to the three kingdoms (animal, vegetable, and mineral) into which nature was divided. The lecturers made use of numerous illustrations, such as charts and pictures, many exhibited on classroom walls, others rolled up like scrolls on cylinders of glazed canvas. The teachers encouraged pupils to ask pertinent questions and provided on-the-spot answers so far as possible out of their storehouse of expert knowledge and experience.

The staff of the New Institution was particularly proud of its accomplishments in the teaching of geography. Owen himself ascribed the greatest educational values to this subject as a means of training children to be open-minded about peoples and ways of living different from their own. He felt that young people who acquired sufficient knowledge concerning such matters from the study of geography would be less inclined to develop prejudices against fellow human beings. For this reason he made the work in geography a prominent feature of the school program, often inviting visitors to sit in on a geography class to observe the pupils reciting information about foreign lands—names of countries and capital cities, facts about customs and manners, locations, physical features, climate, and cultural institutions. A great deal of time was devoted to map work, which frequently became a game, stimulating the pupils' interest, testing their knowledge, and giving them the opportunity to apply the information they had acquired. One child might ask another to locate various places on an unmarked map, and if the child being questioned failed to answer correctly, he had to surrender the pointer to his questioner. In such games the pupils exhibited so much expertise that the geography classes became a highlight of visitors' tours to New Lanark.

The teachers linked history to geography by using illustrated maps to describe the principal events in the history of a nation. Historical facts were arranged in chronological sequence to keep pace with the teacher's discussion of the events depicted in them so that what happened in history was studied in association with geographical locations, resources, and conditions. The pupils memorized numerous historical facts, but not merely as rote exercises, for Owen felt that they would understand and remember them best if an interesting, anecdotal presentation emphasized causes and effects, major occurrences, political and social trends, and the lessons of history.

Vocal and instrumental music and dancing were taught for pure enjoyment as well as for the development of aesthetic standards and values. In music lessons, at the age of five or six years the children studied the names and sounds of the notes, with the help of a large scale printed on canvas, and they memorized the words and melodies of appropriate music. In dancing lessons, which Owen regarded as a most useful means of improving the physical and the emotional well-being of both children and adults, the emphasis was placed upon lively dances, such as Scottish reels, country dances, and quadrilles. The uniforms worn by pupils for dancing and strenuous exercises reflected his consideration for their needs and welfare. These garments, "somewhat resembling the Roman and Highland garb,"[9] were comfortable, allowing free circulation of air, and neat in appearance as well as economical for parents to purchase.

For all subjects in the curriculum the teachers were expected to apply Owen's psychological principles of learning—for example, the principle of step-by-step learning from known facts to the unknown and from simple to more complex information and skills. "They [the children] should first be taught the knowledge of facts, commencing with those which are most familiar to the young mind, and gradually proceeding to the most useful and necessary to be known by the respective individuals in the rank of life in which they are likely to be placed."[10]

New subjects were introduced in outline form; the children were told what material they would be covering; details were omitted until the class fully comprehended the scope and direction of the new information. Rejecting the customary reliance on rote memorization of abstract ideas, Owen insisted that children should understand whatever they study so that they would have something meaningful to remember. He opposed the common practice of rewarding or punishing children as a means of inducing them to memorize (by rote) information or ideas incomprehensible to them. At New Lanark subject matter was taught at an opportune time and in an interesting manner, often with the aid of illustrative anecdotes, so that the pupils would be motivated to absorb and retain the material. Children's questions signalled topics of interest and areas for further instruction. From these indications teachers would plan future lessons. Children's needs were constantly under consideration in Owen's schools. A major principle in lesson planning was "whatever is likely to prove unpleasant or irksome to the children, and is not necessary for the preservation of good order, or for some other useful purpose, should never be required of them. At the same time, whatever is really necessary to the proper regulation of the school, is uniformly but mildly enforced."[11] Always the staff drew a sharp distinction between learning through mere repetition and the more basic and useful process of comprehension with retention and recall.

III   Religion in the Curriculum

The numerous church schools of Great Britain were intent upon making certain that the pupils read, understood, and accepted their respective denominational interpretations of the Bible, and most people condemned teachers as irreverent who failed to teach those dogmas. Although Owen also favored Biblical instruction, he regarded the conflicting interpretations as distortions or corruptions of the original Scriptures, a view he had held since childhood when he was encouraged to read religious and biographical books in the libraries of Methodist spinsters in Newtown who attempted to win the boy over to their faith. Wide reading did not alter but seemed to strengthen his skeptical attitude toward the various religions so often at odds with one another, an attitude persisting throughout his lifetime and expressed on one occasion in his comment that all religions are "geographical insanities."[12]

According to Owen, members of religious sects were all victims of distortion: "The Jews believe the Christians to speak the language of insanity—the Christians believe the Hindoos to talk this language—the Hindoos believe the Mahomedans to be insane—and, thus, each superstition blinds the mental faculties of its victims, only permitting them to perceive the gross irrationality of all other superstitutions."[13]

His son Robert Dale Owen described him as a Deist and also as a "free-thinking Unitarian."[14]

Eventually Owen proclaimed his firm belief that the only valid religion is truth, proposing that

We abandon all the false religions that have been forced upon the human race. . . .
We now adopt the only religion which can be true, because it is derived immediately from the unchangeable and everlasting laws of nature, which never lie, or deceive the human race. The basis of this Religion of Truth . . . is the knowledge that the laws of nature have given the power to adult man, so to control the mental faculties and physical powers of his infant, as to force it to receive error, however absurd and inconsistent, or to imbibe truth only, . . .[15]

By publicly expounding his belief in a secular form of religion, Owen alienated many influential people who misunderstood his program of religious education. Yet he reassured parents that if their religion were the true one, it would prevail more steadfastly in view of the children's general knowledge of universal truths. In fact, he accepted the Bible as the basis for the course of study in religion and instructed the teachers at New Lanark not only to teach the Scriptures in a nondenominational context but also, since the parents demanded it, to include the catechism. Major emphasis was placed upon teaching the moral principles of Christianity, for Owen concluded that the pupils should not have to decide about the validity of denominational doctrines until they were old enough to do so wisely. He warned that since children could not understand the precepts of religion, they would quickly become bored if forced to memorize meaningless dogma. As Owen did not approve of rote memorization in academic subjects, neither did he advocate it in religious instruction. He would have preferred to act in accordance with the interests of truth by informing the pupils about the various opposing arguments of religion.

Owen no doubt anticipated that many of his students, having been trained to reason carefully about ideas, would adhere to his own faith in truth as the only rational religion. He therefore urged abandonment of the attempt to teach religious dogmas in the schools, stating that their elimination from the curriculum whenever parents gave their consent would result in a purified, benevolent, universal, true religion.

My efforts have been, and will be directed to secure the interests of true religion, and to establish it permanently throughout the world. I well know, and am now competent to prove, that the real enemies to truth, to genuine religion, and to the happiness of mankind, among all people, are those parts of every religion that are in direct and palpable contradiction to existing facts, and which have been added to pure and undefiled religion, either by weak, mistaken, or by designing men. Withdraw these from the Christian system, and then it will become a religion of universal benevolence, competent to make, and it will make, men rational and happy. Let but this change be effected, and I will become a Christian indeed.[16]

IV   *Adult Education*

Experiments in adult education had been rare occurrences when in 1816 Robert Owen organized the New Institution. In 1789 a few adult classes had been conducted in Birmingham; in 1798 William Singleton and Samuel Fox had established a school for adults at Nottingham; and in 1812 William Smith had founded a school in Bristol to teach adults to read. Owen's educational program for adults broke new ground. It was a diversified, informal program of parent education, including counseling in academic and skill subjects, discussion groups, and instruction in home management. The evening classes were open to all adults as well as to the adolescent graduates of the New Institution, who were encouraged to continue their education. Most of the adult classes were informal, inasmuch as people who had worked hard all day in the mills were usually too tired to undertake formal instruction. Nevertheless, adults were helped to master at their own pace practical subjects such as reading, writing, accounting, and sewing. Group discussions of common problems in child psychology, consumer economics, and family living were among the most popular features of the adult education program. Often the school building was used for concerts, dancing, and community meetings in which problems and projects for the common good could be discussed.

Owen knew that education for adults could be enhanced not only within the schools but also outside the school buildings. The adults in New Lanark were constantly being reeducated: by their participation in beneficial civic enterprises and the good examples set by community leaders; by their peers in the factory through the influence of social pressure and prestige, as in the reactions to the silent monitor; and by their own properly educated children whose ideas and correct habits improved the home environment. It was therefore only natural for Owen to wish that the mothers of these children could reduce the number of hours they worked in the mills and devote most of their time to caring for their infants and attending to the domestic needs of the family. He was not too sanguine about the prospect of quickly attaining perfection in this or any other aspect of social and educational reform, for he knew that the achievement of fundamental changes in the attitudes and behavior patterns of adults would be a difficult, gradual process.

CHAPTER 8

Owen Compared with Other Educators

OWEN claimed that similarities between his work and that of contemporary educators were either coincidental or the results of attempts on their parts to duplicate his educational innovations. Nonetheless, testifying in 1816 before a parliamentary committee investigating the education of pauper children, he stated that his schools combined the best features of other experimental systems, such as those of the educational reformers Andrew Bell and Joseph Lancaster. His educational program, said Owen, "gives great facility to children to acquire a knowledge of reading, writing, and arithmetic, and the girls sewing,"[1] adding that the children learned these subjects more quickly and retained them more permanently than had ever been possible in traditional schools. Similar claims were made by Bell and Lancaster for their own systems which antedated but differed markedly from Owen's in methodology. Other leading contemporary educators included Johann Heinrich Pestalozzi, Philipp Emanuel von Fellenberg, Johann Friedrich Herbart, and Friedrich Wilhelm August Froebel, each of whom expounded many ideas shared by Owen, although the latter developed his educational philosophy and methods independently as a means of fulfilling his visionary ethical and socialist objectives.

I The Monitorial System

Andrew Bell and Joseph Lancaster utilized a monitorial system of education in which older pupils who had mastered assigned units of subject matter attempted to teach the same material to younger ones. Owen analyzed the methods of these two educators and, although he deplored their reliance upon memoriter learning (which underemphasized understanding and reasoning), he encouraged both men in their efforts and contributed funds to their enterprises. Despite his critical attitude, his assistance was gratefully accepted, and he was chosen to be the guest speaker at a testimonial dinner for Lancaster.

Bell and Lancaster each claimed to have originated the monitorial system (probably developed by them independently), but their method was not new, for the Hindus had long made use of it in the schools of India, Comenius (1592 - 1671) had recommended it, and in England John Brinsley had proposed it as early as 1612. Chevalier Paulet organized a school (1790) in Paris that utilized a monitorial procedure, but France during the ensuing revolutionary era employed the method in only a few schools. The British experiments of Bell and Lancaster, however, came at the right place and time to help popularize the expansion of education, for which an economical means of teaching was desired. In Great Britain the cost of individual instruction by tutor or teacher was too high, the practical results too poor, to permit much expansion until the method of mutual instruction by pupils themselves awakened popular interest in providing means of religious and secular education for the masses.

II *Andrew Bell (1753 - 1832)*

The Anglican clergyman Andrew Bell published a report in 1797 describing a monitorial system he had been using in his school in Madras, India. (Lancaster conducted his first comparable experiment in 1798.) Later Bell became the director of monitorial schools financed by an organization founded in 1811, the National Society for Promoting the Education of the Poor in the Principles of the Established Church, of which the Archbishop of Canterbury was president. The curriculum of these schools was restricted mainly to religion, the three Rs, and vocational training, for the churchmen believed that the poor should not be educated above their station in life. Bell advocated a scheme of national education, with religious instruction as its foundation, which would be organized and controlled by the Church of England. The Bell system was utilized in thousands of schools throughout England and in foreign countries but was eventually discarded as certain defects of the method (such as its overemphasis upon drill and memoriter learning) became apparent.

Owen stated that he contributed funds to assist Bell (as well as Lancaster) "to make a beginning in this country to give even the mite of instruction to the poor which their respective systems proposed to do, because I trusted that a beginning might be made to lead on gradually to something substantial and permanently beneficial to society."[2] But Owen's program was based upon fundamental objectives far different from those of Bell. Whereas the latter felt that education should not become a means of improving the social status of the poor, Owen insisted that his instructional program would be the best method of enabling individuals to attain a higher standard of living and would ennoble and remake human nature itself. Although Owen was willing to compromise by teaching the catechism requested by parents, he rejected the dogmas and extremely narrow curriculum of Bell and the established church. Furthermore, Owen, opposing the large classes and military discipline advocated by Bell, felt that good education could be provided only in small groups by teachers endowed with sympathy and love for the children in their care, children entitled to happiness, cherished as potentially superior human beings.

III   Joseph Lancaster (1778 - 1838)

When the young English Quaker Joseph Lancaster organized a school for poor children in Southwark, London, he found that he could not himself instruct the hundred or more pupils who had enrolled, also that he had no funds to pay additional teachers. He solved the problem by teaching older children, or "monitors," who in turn taught the younger ones. Thus Lancaster independently devised the same monitorial system which Bell had already utilized in the Madras school.

Lancaster's school enrolled hundreds of pupils and attracted so much favorable attention that many similar schools were soon formed in England. His first school, which became a model for others to follow, was converted into a teacher-training school to prepare teachers for the new method of instruction. But Lancaster was a poor manager and got himself so deeply into debt that to rescue him a few philanthropists in 1808 formed "The Royal Lancasterian Institution," which was later reorganized as "The British and Foreign School Society" to support elementary schools and teacher-training institutions. (Many of the elementary schools and some of the normal schools remained in operation until 1870, at which time they were incorporated into the English system of public education.) Lancaster left England in 1818 to assist in the organization of monitorial schools in the United States where the small one-teacher schools had become inefficient and wasteful. Again his poor management got him into personal difficulties, but the movement spread and did much to awaken nationwide interest in public education. Eventually, however, as the drawbacks of monitorial schools, their excessive formalism and overemphasis on drill, became apparent, and as the American people became more willing to support public schools, the sounder methods advocated by other educators, such as Pestalozzi, Herbart, and Froebel, displaced the Lancastrian procedures. By mid-century most of the schools in the United States had given up the monitorial method of instruction.

Owen objected to the excessive order and discipline of Lancaster's schools, to the drillmaster attitude toward children, to the ranking of pupils on the basis of memorized subject matter (the children wore numbered badges indicating their rank in each subject), to severe punishment for misbehavior, to inflexible oral commands by monitors, and to their constant surveillance to make certain that each child learned every unit of information perfectly. The absence of meaningful learning, a basic deficiency of the Lancasterian method which had quickly become apparent to Owen, was aptly described in 1845 in a report of the Council on Education. That report referred to "boys about 11½ years old, reading with ease, but not much intelligence; writing from dictation, so as to give the sense of a passage, but without any regard to punctuation, or any practical knowledge of grammar; with more or less facility in working the ordinary rules of arithmetic to proportion or practice, but with little or no insight into its principles."[3] Nevertheless, Owen arranged for Lancaster to meet with influential potential backers in Scotland and commented that he had been Lancaster's "first and most confided-in patron as long as he remained in England."[4]

Lancaster's curriculum was broader, his materials and methods

more highly developed, than Bell's. Although the Lancasterians
taught the Bible with considerable attention to generally accepted
doctrines, they agreed with Owen's view in many instances that
there should be no favoritism shown to the interpretations of any
particular religious sect. This policy was a natural one since these
schools were supported by dissenters, not by the established church
which preferred Bell's curriculum. Both Lancaster and Bell used a
desk covered with sand for teaching handwriting. Lancaster took
great pains to make all procedures and materials as economical and
efficient as possible, providing a single text in very large type on a
subject so that a group of many pupils could read from it, dictating
spelling words to as many as five hundred boys who were required
to write each word immediately on their slates, and in similar ways
achieving unprecedented quantitative results but generally without
regard for the psychological powers and needs of the pupils. The
system was of course directly contrary to Owen's emphasis upon
happy learning experiences, spontaneity, and the pupil's interests,
skills, and stage of intellectual development.

IV   *Johann Heinrich Pestalozzi (1746 - 1827)*

Pestalozzi admired the philosophy of education expounded by
Jean Jacques Rousseau in the class novel *Émile* and attempted to
carry out Rousseau's ideas in Switzerland, beginning in 1774 with
instruction of poor Swiss children at Neuhof, continuing with experiments at Stanz, Burgdorf, and Hofwyl, and culminating in
pioneering education during a period of twenty years at the
renowned Institute in Yverdon. (Similar attempts had been made
with mixed results in Dessau, Germany, by Johann Bernard
Basedow, whose emphasis on nature study, handicrafts, object
teaching, home geography, child interests, and life experience as
the basis for educational methods became influential not only in
Germany but also in France and Switzerland, and was further
developed by other great educators, including Pestalozzi.) The initial experiment at Neuhof was a financial failure, declared
bankrupt in 1780, but Pestalozzi observed the beneficent results of
providing instruction in practical skills of farming, home
maintenance, needlework, and spinning and weaving cotton, while
at the same time teaching boys and girls to read and memorize the

Bible and to write. The children appeared healthier, better behaved, and also more competent in their work, conversation, and mastery of academic fundamentals. In 1781 Pestalozzi set forth his principal pedagogical ideas in *Leonard and Gertrude*, a novel relating how a new type of education reformed a Swiss village.

Although he rejected the teaching of denominational dogmas as the basis for schooling, just as Owen did, Pestalozzi felt that education should be fundamentally a religious enterprise because all of human destiny is derived from God, man owes his inner goodness and morality to divine guidance, and ethical and religious doctrines are identical derivations from the Scriptures. Owen, especially in his later years, made a sharp distinction between the religious tenets of the churches, subject to conflicting and often contradictory interpretations, and the principles of morality which, though accepted by adherents to Christianity, are valid truths in themselves and should therefore be taught as rational choices irrespective of, and independent of, any particular religious persuasion.

In his autobiography (published in 1857) Owen recalled that he had been generally critical of Pestalozzi's procedures but favorable to the basic aims of the great Swiss educator, of whom he wrote: "His theory was good, but his means and experience were very limited, and his principles were those of the old system."[5] Yet he shared Pestalozzi's views that employers should assume responsibility for the education of their young workers and all other children of the poor, that every child should be educated in knowledge and skills necessary for a vocation and civic duties, that observation of nature, sense impressions, individual judgment, and understanding of subject matter should replace the memorization of "mere senseless words" in learning, that self-discipline, self-expression (using conversation instead of grammar rules in teaching language), and child experience with nature and objects would develop children's inner powers and moral character and thus regenerate society. There was no disagreement about the ideal relationship between teacher and pupils, especially the need for mutual understanding, sympathy, and respect for the individual. Both educators agreed that the child should be taught only when interested and ready for learning, that education should progress from the known to the unknown, and that subject matter should be adapted to the needs of the individual. But Owen, who visited

Pestalozzi in Switzerland in 1818, resented the latter's retention of certain objectionable methods of instruction, such as the use of monitors as teachers and considerable reliance upon memorization through constant repetition of information, practices that had been rejected at New Lanark. It is true that Pestalozzi utilized many verbalistic and memoriter methods, even though he often vehemently criticized such methods. Perhaps the fundamental difference between the two educators is the fact that Pestalozzi was enthusiastic about the value of the child's sense experience and self-expression, not as an essential ingredient of self-education, but only as an instrument for achieving results considered desirable by the teacher, whereas Owen felt that intellectual activity, life experience, is itself the essence of education. Owen's rejection of all forms of verbalism and symbolism may explain why he concluded that Pestalozzi had retained too many of the principles of the old system of education. Pestalozzi was ever willing to experiment with new approaches and procedures in teaching, sometimes inconsistent with his own basic principles but always stimulating educational philosophers and teachers to consider new approaches to child development. His innovative combination of agricultural and industrial training with nature study and subject teaching based upon observation, work with objects, and children's interests, was further implemented by his friend and associate Fellenberg at Hofwyl, Switzerland.

V   *Philipp Emanuel von Fellenberg (1771 - 1844)*

Fellenberg was a wealthy philanthropist who applied many of the ideas promulgated by Pestalozzi and Owen, with special emphasis upon manual activity and vocational instruction, particularly in farming and industrial trades, for children in all ranks of society. Fellenberg's intention was not to revolutionize the social structure but only to educate the masses so that the poor, middle, and upper classes alike would achieve moral and material progress, mutual respect and cooperation. Doing plus thinking carefully about what is being done was the primary method of learning espoused at Hofwyl, Fellenberg's school, which for several decades served as a model for multitudes of schools in Switzerland, Germany, France, England, and the United States, all of which countries developed extensive programs of agricultural and industrial training. Such programs have continued to the present, often advocated as the best available means both for the reeducation of children and adults and for the reduction of juvenile delinquency, crime, and recividism—familiar themes reiterated by parents, teachers, and community leaders in our own times. In the principal areas of national education, Fellenberg's curriculum for boys (with preparation for farming, blacksmithing, carpentry, tailoring, and the like) and for girls (including the household arts) offered, in addition to vocational training, instruction in academic subjects: the three Rs, music, mathematics, science, geography, history, physical culture, and religious studies. Fellenberg's highly successful enterprise and ideas (even after his death in 1844 his influence spread widely) continued to stimulate interest in educational opportunities for orphans, physically handicapped children, and convicts.

Owen, who agreed enthusiastically with Fellenberg's major philanthropic and pedagogical objectives and methods, commented that the school at Hofwyl was "two or three steps in advance of any I had yet seen in England or on the Continent."[6] But there was one fundamental difference between the programs of New Lanark and Hofwyl, for Fellenberg never advocated the use of education for the purpose of eliminating social classes or the reorganizing of society into a cooperative socialistic community. The rich would be taught to respect the poor, and vice versa. Although he recommended vocational and moral training for all, irrespective of rank, Fellenberg prepared his students to accept their station in life without protest, whereas Owen envisioned an egalitarian society of community-minded citizens. In other respects, however, Owen approved of Fellenberg as "a man of no ordinary mould,—possessing rare administrative talent, and a good knowledge of human nature . . . alive to its many errors and defects."[7] After visiting Hofwyl in 1818, he was so favorably impressed by Fellenberg's program that he chose that school for the education of his two eldest sons, Robert Dale (sixteen) and William Dale (fourteen), who had previously been instructed in their home by "well-selected"[8] governesses and private tutors in several foreign languages and various customary academic subjects.

Robert Dale Owen reported an enrollment of one hundred students at Hofwyl. The Owens were the only students from

England (the others were from many European countries) and, as sons of a famous father, received special attention from Fellenberg, but ordinarily a student's social rank and religion were not taken into consideration in relationships among students and faculty. Fellenberg himself was called *Pflegevater* (foster father) by the boys, all of whom enjoyed a close, affectionate, mutually respectful association with him. Moreover, the students drew up their own constitution and were completely self-governing, with rules and regulations applied equally to sons of royalty and to the rank and file, a highly successful honor system enforced by peer pressure. Classes were small (ten to fifteen members), taught by a staff of twenty-five to thirty instructors. The curriculum included Greek, Latin, French, German, history, natural philosophy, chemistry, mechanics, mathematics, drawing, music, riding, fencing, and non-denominational religious sermons. The entire program of work and diversified studies, combined with self-discipline, democratic self-government, and warm human relationships was perfectly consistent with the objectives of New Lanark and Owen's philosophy of education.

VI   *Johann Friedrich Herbart (1776 - 1841)*

The influential German professor Herbart visited Pestalozzi's school in Burgdorf, Switzerland, in 1799 and commended the ideas and methods of the Swiss educator. But Herbart did not adhere to the assumption by Pestalozzi (and by Owen) that education is a process of developing separate innate mental faculties. On the contrary, Herbart felt that the mind is a single entity which can be directed by teachers through effective instruction so that each pupil will become a good citizen and morally sound person. This aim could be achieved, he said, by studying man in the total natural and social environment and then providing instruction in carefully worked-out steps. Thus the child would understand and assimilate the most useful knowledge, attitudes, and ideas. Herbart advocated the scientific study of children's natures and the use of subject matter to insure the development of high moral character and civic responsibility.

John Dewey pointed out that Herbart made teaching a "conscious business with a definite aim and procedure . . . abolished the notion of ready-made faculties . . . trained by exercise upon any sort of material, and made attention to concrete subject matter . . . all-important."[9] Dewey's comment expressed a basic criticism that could well have been made by Owen, namely, that Herbart underemphasized the activity of the learner, who must himself interpret and react to information and experience. For Herbart, the task of the teacher is to organize knowledge and present it in suitable steps to be absorbed and understood by the pupil. For Owen, as for Rousseau, Pestalozzi, and Dewey, what the child does of his own volition, spontaneously, naturally, is the most significant requisite for personal growth and for the development of moral character, and education should be an active, enjoyable, useful experience shared by the individual, his companions, parents, and teachers.

Herbart's fundamental premises were: (1) the human mind can be developed intellectually by arousal of interest and systematic experience in interpreting, combining, and organizing ideas; and (2) human character can be uplifted through the study and acquisition of moral ideals. Owen would not have disagreed with these premises, but he would have added his own visionary reformist principles. In fact, Herbart established a new type of formalistic education, attempting to psychologize learning by delineating five formal steps: (1) preparation for learning: readiness, or apperceptive base; (2) presentation of new material and ideas; (3) association of the new with the old subject matter in the learner's mind; (4) derivation of new relationships or general principles to be understood and remembered; and (5) application of the new facts and principles to problems and tasks of the learner. Herbart thereby made a great advance in the direction of scientific investigation of the learning process, whereas Owen depended upon his own experience with and insight into the psychological needs of children and the social needs of the community. Owen was temperamentally opposed to excessive formalism which could be used to enforce autocratic education and government, and he favored the humane spontaneity and cooperation more suited to a democratic, though perhaps at times less efficient, society.

VII *Friedrich Wilhelm August Froebel (1782 - 1852)*

Froebel originated the idea of the kindergarten as a spiritual garden in which the child fulfills his potential nature (based on natural instincts and impulses) through play, motor expression, guided self-activity, social cooperation, and individual development, which he mystically explained as a creative, evolving blossoming of divine goodness innate in every person. Education must be regarded, said Froebel, not as preparation for life, but as an active process of living in a purified, miniature society. The young child is given cubes, cylinders, tablets, sticks, rings, paper, sand, clay, and other materials which he can manipulate and build into objects, forms, designs, and patterns. Individual and group projects requiring initiative, imagination, and manual dexterity, supplemented by stories, legends, fairy tales, and fables, become the central method of Froebel's kindergarten.

In his advocacy of infant education, Owen was several years in advance of Froebel, who began his first experimental program in 1816, the same year that Owen opened the New Institution for the Formation of Character. Both educators attributed social evils to incorrect methods of education and agreed that the new approaches advocated by Rousseau and Pestalozzi could develop in the child moral sensitivity, good habits of conduct, social cooperation, and a better understanding of nature and humanity. Froebel differed sharply from Owen on basic issues, however, as in Froebel's assumptions that children are innately good, that the mother is the best teacher of her own children, and that mystical religious ideals should guide the choice of educational procedures. Owen believed that children are innately neither good nor bad, that they should be removed at an early age from parental influence, and that social change, not religious aims, is the best foundation of effective education—social change to achieve the ideal socialist community. Owen and Froebel agreed that child activity, spontaneity, self-discipline, self-expression, and social cooperation should replace traditional rote memorization and books as the core of the learning process.

VIII   *Owen's Pedagogical Contribution*

Differentiating his educational philosophy (which he had worked out independently on the basis of his own industrial, philanthropic, and personal life experiences and his school experiments) from the ideas of other famous contemporary educators, Owen concluded that the latter were concerned mainly about specific methods of teaching subject matter and skills. In his judgment, children, even if they had been taught these things well, could still acquire bad habits and become "irrational" or irresponsible adults. His educational system, he insisted, would develop the rational ability and moral character potentially within every child and thereby achieve good citizenship and a better society. "Reading and writing are merely instruments by which knowledge, either true or false, may be imparted; and, when given to children, are of little comparative value, unless they are also taught how to make a proper use of them."[10]

The best methods of teaching information to children would therefore be futile unless accompanied by instruction in correct reasoning and by constant guidance to insure the formation of moral behavior patterns. Granted that certain methods of teaching might be effective aids to education, nevertheless, in his opinion, the content of the information digested by the child—the truth about the self, nature, and society—must take precedence over the formal design, the specific procedures, of the educational process.

The *worst* manner may be applied to give the *best* instruction, and the *best* manner to give the *worst* instruction. Were the real importance of both to be estimated by numbers, the manner of instruction may be compared to one, and the matter of instruction to millions: the first is the means only; the last, the end to be accomplished by those means.[11]

Consequently, the best of teachers would accomplish little by teaching the same old, erroneous information to his pupils.

Owen was unique among his contemporary educators in demanding simultaneous reforms in education and in government (as Rousseau had done), reforms to be applied for the benefit of infants, of older children and adults working in factories, of parents and homeowners—reforms designed to remake the moral character of the entire community. Opposition to his ideas came from many parents who disliked the idea of being separated from their children during school hours, or who needed the money their children could earn in the mills, and from poor adults who had been conditioned to accept the proposition that education should be restricted to children in the upper strata of society. Owen appealed to parents to show proof of love for their children:

Parents cannot render their children a more substantial and permanent service than by placing them in a situation where they would be trained from
their earliest years to regard each of their fellows as a friend, to love him,
and to seek to do him good—where no motives to envy, jealousy, and contention, would be instilled into their young minds. . . .Would it not be the
highest proof of affection which parents could show for their offspring, to
train and educate them upon these principles?—and can it be conceived
that children would love their parents the less, who had bestowed upon
them such a blessing?[12]

Owen's unprecedented appeals and arguments were effective
contributions to the spread and improvement of education,
stimulating the demand for infant schools and trained teachers, especially for women teachers of very young children, and
strengthening the faith of parents in high moral and social ideals as
the foundation of education, as the only means of enabling their
children to become useful members of the community. In all his
progressive views and practical programs, Owen reiterated one central idea—that the attainment of happiness is the beginning and
end of all instruction, a goal to be understood, appreciated, and
sought by children and adults in the community. Happiness could
not be achieved, he said, until the people could provide "a really
good character for all from birth to death"[13] and "a superfluity of
real wealth at all times for all."[14] Proper education for the masses
would be the means of elevating the character of all peoples and ultimately attaining universal happiness for mankind.

CHAPTER 9

The Old System of Education

IN Great Britain early in the nineteenth century, new economic and social forces speeded the process of social and educational change. Factors conducive to change included the political unrest stimulated in part by the French Revolution, the rapid expansion of manufacturing accompanied by growing decline and distress in agriculture, the progress of science and invention, increasing replacement of hand labor by machines, and advances in democratic government and in communication and public opinion, particularly through the press and public meetings, all of which created a demand for wider educational opportunities. As the nation prospered industrially, social problems multiplied while conservative leaders resisted the extension of education to the masses, fearful that it would increase discontent and incite the lower classes to rebellion. Many leaders of industry dreaded the cost of educating the multitude, and churchmen preferred to maintain the status quo in education, which meant a narrow curriculum provided by religious schools to teach the people to read the Bible.

I Scope and Purpose of Education

Educational facilities had long been available to the upper classes out of which came the leaders of religious, economic, professional, and political institutions. Tutors and endowed schools for the children of the well-to-do taught the traditional subjects, such as religion, Latin and the classics, science, philosophy, foreign languages, and techniques of the learned professions. Even the young women in the élite classes enjoyed many educational advantages. Owen reported that when he became their guardian, after the death of his father-in-law, his four sisters-in-law, for example, had already received a religious education, which he regarded as insufficient preparation for adult life, and therefore he sent them to board "in private and select"[1] schools in London, finishing schools to train young women in matters of social comportment; the schools he selected also devoted considerable attention to academic studies. Wealthy parents usually arranged for tutors in the home to instruct their sons whom they would eventually send off either on a grand tour of the Continent or to study at Oxford or Cambridge.

The middle class, growing rapidly in numbers and infuence, owing to the surge of industrialization, endowed numerous private schools for their sons. Education for the poor was still regarded as a charitable undertaking of dubious value at best. Children in the lower classes of British society could hope only to become apprentices or domestic servants; it was generally assumed that learning would be wasted if made available to the common people, that the poor were destined for a lifetime of manual labor in mills or factories and needed no education for such a career. With further progress of industrialization, however, vocational schools were organized to train workers needed by the factories. A major new development came with the monitorial schools which at one time enrolled over a million pupils. There were also large numbers enrolled in Sunday schools, church schools, and other charity schools. Nevertheless, only a minority of poor children attended any school whatever, and they received instruction of such low quality as to be little better than nothing at all. The great majority were sent off to work in mills or factories to earn the meager salaries urgently needed in the home. In fact, many parents purposely had large families in order to supplement the family income. Boys and girls from infancy worked like adults and were in fact looked upon as miniature adults, not to be pampered, protected, or educated, but required to assume the same burdens and responsibilities as adults in a harsh, increasingly industrialized and competitive community. Even in appearance tiny children resembled adults, wearing similar clothing and imitating adult mannerisms. The children at New Lanark were the rare exception, supplied with special uniforms, for Owen treated them as children, as individuals entitled to a measure of ease and comfort during their exercises, dances, and other activities.

Owen protested against the limited number of educational opportunities for the poor, and also against the inefficient methods of instruction used in the schools for the upper classes whose children, he claimed, were quite often not much better off educationally than the poor who attended no school. The teaching of religion, the rote memorization of inaccurate information, and the maintenance of discipline by means of severe physical punishment seemed to Owen especially harmful, the end result being to "produce a most imperfect character, physical and mental, in all."[2] For several decades he preached his gospel that it would be far easier and more economical to provide good education that would create a more competent and morally superior human being. "By a right education and direction of all our faculties and powers, with much less cost of capital, labour, and good feeling, a very superior character might be insured to each individual."[3]

Many infant schools were organized in the United Kingdom, owing in part to the work of Owen and Buchanan; of Samuel Wilderspin (1792 - 1866) who wrote and lectured in favor of such schools; of David Stowe (1793 - 1864), founder of infant schools in Scotland; and of two famous disciples of Pestalozzi, namely, the Reverend Charles Mayo (1792 - 1846) and James Pierrepont Greaves (1777 - 1842) who helped to make teaching procedures more flexible, informal, and enjoyable for children. But even in Scotland, home of the New Lanark schools, where social class distinctions were not so sharp as in England, opportunities for the children of the poor remained extremely limited.

II   *Religious Schools and Charity Schools*

During the eighteenth century the principal types of elementary schools in England had been the parish schools, endowed schools, dame schools, Sunday Schools, and the charity schools organized by the Society for Promoting Christian Knowledge. Some of these schools remained prominent early in the nineteenth century, at which time the religious schools, the monitorial schools of Bell and Lancaster, the Sunday schools, and the infant schools, patterned after Owen's experiments, accounted for much of the increased enrollment. Many of the schools taught little more than reading and writing, with emphasis on reading the Bible. In 1832 the Reform Act enlarged the suffrage, and Parliament soon began to provide limited funds for the construction of school buildings. Enlightened leaders knew that the poor would have to be taught to read if they were ever to become intelligent, informed citizens and competent workers.

The Church of England was not at all enthusiastic about the extension of education to the masses, fearing that nondenominational religious or secular instruction by Dissenters or by the state would weaken Anglican authority and influence. Dissenters used their schools as means of converting youth to unpopular religious beliefs, with catechetical memorization as the core of the curriculum. Lancaster, who was himself a Quaker, began teaching in a school organized to teach children the basic tenets of his sect. Owen appealed in vain to Bell and Lancaster to open their monitorial schools to children of all creeds. Competition between the Bell schools of the Established Church and the Lancasterian schools of the Dissenters impelled both sides to found new schools and thus rapidly expanded the educational opportunities of the poor. In 1820 there were about one thousand schools founded by the religious societies of England, about 90 per cent of them affiliated with the Church of England; by 1840 the number of such schools has increased to 4,600, of which about 75 per cent were affiliated with the Church of England. In addition, in 1820 there were more than five thousand Sunday schools, with a total enrollment of about 500,000 pupils which by mid-century increased to 2,500,000 pupils. In 1820 Lord Brougham estimated that there were also about 430,000 pupils enrolled in privately endowed charity schools. Many of the private charity schools rarely taught much more than reading, and some charged a small fee.

Since there was no state supervision of the schools, qualifications of teachers varied widely. Schools of the Society for Promoting Christian Knowledge required applicants for teaching positions to be twenty-five years or older, members of the Church of England, and competent in writing, arithmetic, Christian religion, and classroom discipline. These were indeed exceptional requirements, for the majority of schoolmasters during the nineteenth century were men and women who had become unemployed or had failed in some other occupation, many of them ignorant people and callous disciplinarians. Charles Dickens commented on the teachers of his day: "Any man who had proved his unfitness for any other occupation in life, was free, without examination or qualification, to open a school anywhere; . . . schoolmasters, as a race, were the blockheads and impostors who might naturally be expected to spring from such a state of things."[4] Dickens was referring to the numerous privately managed schools organized to meet the demand for more education while making a handsome profit for the proprietors, but the situation was not much better in the nonprofit religious and charity schools.

The dismal picture that Dickens painted of one boarding school in the late 1830s understated the deadly rote learning, rigid discipline, and rank injustices perpetrated upon children in most of the schools of his time. The school he described in *Nicholas Nickleby* was a battlefield for the two teachers, Mr. and Mrs. Sqeers, and their charges whom they whipped for miniscule offenses.

Now, the fact was, that both Mr. and Mrs. Sqeers viewed the boys in the light of their proper and natural enemies; or, in other words, they held and considered that their business and profession was to get as much from every boy as could by possibility be screwed out of him. . . . The only difference between them was, that Mrs. Sqeers waged war against the enemy openly and fearlessly, and that Sqeers covered his rascality, even at home, with a spice of his habitual deceit.[5]

Not surprisingly, Dickens found no "boisterous play, or hearty mirth"[6] in the classroom, but only apathy, lack of spirit. No wonder that children of the poor, even when offered the choice, usually preferred to go to work in mill or factory rather than suffer abuse at school.

III *Owen's Analysis of the Old System*

Owen agitated for free, nondenominational, public education. He condemned the biased instruction and dreary regimens provided for the poor by voluntary institutions. His remedial proposals were directly contrary to the practices of the old system of education. To him it seemed imperative that not only a minority, but all children from all ranks in society should be taught the same basic subjects, such as reading, writing, and arithmetic, and as much more of knowledge and skill as they could learn, in a healthful environment by highly qualified teachers so that every child would be given "the best education from infancy to maturity."[7] Even the monitorial schools, which he at first encouraged as a start on the road to expanded educational opportunities for the poor, employed untrained students as teachers in many situations, utilized ineffective methods of instruction requiring memorization of frequently incorrect or misunderstood information, and perpetuated authoritarian, antagonistic human relationships. Numerous industrial schools, privately owned, were organized near the mills and factories to train children for work in industry, but the owners of these schools were interested primarily in profits from fees and the sale of products manufactured by the pupils. Many parents preferred to send their sons off to work instead of paying fees for exploitative training programs. Owen pleaded in vain for a publicly supported, state-supervised, new system of universal education. Not until 1847 was a bill passed (against vehement opposition by the religious societies) to establish a national system of education, and it was not until 1870 that an act to establish a system of elementary schools fully under state control was made into law.

Owen contrasted the hodgepodge of ineffective educational institutions in England with his own proposed system of national education:

The truth is that the great principle on which the new system rests, is directly opposed to that on which the old society has been founded: . . . The one generates in man anger and irritation, because his fellow man differs from him in sentiments, habits, and feelings. The other instructs how men are necessarily made to differ in color, in language, in habits, in sentiments, in religion, in feeling, and in conduct, and thereby implants in every one the principle of universal charity, benevolence, and kindness, and withdraws all anger from the human constitution. The one separates man from man, individualizing the human race, . . . and thus generates and fosters all the inferior motives and bad passions and actions which have ever pervaded society. The other forms man at once into a rational being; and, by removing every cause of dislike and jealousy, prepares . . . to unite him with his fellows, . . . in one general system of action for their mutual benefit. In short, the one is, in reality, an imaginary notion, which has ever been impressed in infancy on the mind of the human race, in direct opposition to every known fact; . . . While the other is a principle derived from experience, in unison with all facts, past and present: a principle which deprecates all war and violence, and punishment of every kind; . . . the one being the cause of all happiness to man, the other of all misery.[8]

Opponents of Owen's proposal for a national state-controlled system of universal education feared that state regulation "would place a dangerous power in the hands of the ministers of the Crown."[9] They asserted that the central government would be tempted to abuse its authority and impair the rights and privileges traditionally vested in established religious and financial institutions. Owen insisted, however, that only his proposed system of education could meet the needs of the entire population, that it was the responsibility of the central government to provide relief for the poor and ignorant masses, and that all society would benefit from a national system of education. "Train up a child in the way he should go," he said, "and when he is old he will not depart from it."[10] A national system of education, properly designed and administered, would not restrict but rather enlarge the liberty of individuals, since children would learn to use freedom wisely, seeking the benefit of the community, and would develop sympathy for their companions "and a sincere good-will for every individual of the human race."[11] A new society more in harmony with the needs and potentialities of human nature would eventually replace the old society. Owen predicted that universal education such as he proposed would enable people everywhere "to reside in a society whose laws, institutions, and arrangements, well organized and well governed, are all in unison with the laws of human nature."[12] It seemed to him that the old social and educational systems had failed to develop the moral character and potential achievements of the people, that his proposed humane, cooperative, rational systems constituted the only alternatives worthy of serious consideration.

CHAPTER 10

New Harmony

IN 1824, at a time when Owen's experiments seemed to have been developed as far as possible at New Lanark, where the residents were, Owen complained, merely his employees, subject to the whims of their employer, Owen was offered the opportunity to begin his experiments in education and communal living again in a new environment.

About a decade earlier the socialistic religious sect known as the Rappites, after their founder George Rapp (1757 - 1847), had left their communistic community (Harmonie) in Pennsylvania and migrated to Indiana where they settled along the banks of the Wabash River. They prospered in their idealistic community, which they named New Harmonie (later known as New Harmony). They manufactured high-quality woolens and leather goods as well as producing diversified agricultural goods. After ten years of successful industry and trade, however, the Rappites, who were strict celibates, decided to return to Pennsylvania, and consequently determined to sell New Harmonie by placing advertisements in British and American journals. The advertisements described New Harmony as consisting of "3000 acres . . . under fence, and in a high state of cultivation, twelve acres . . . vineyards, covering the hills, thirty-five acres of orchard . . . planted with fourteen hundred apple and pear trees, with sundry peach orchards in full bearing, producing many thousand bushels of the choicest fruit." The town was said to be "the highly esteemed and much celebrated town and settlement of Harmony, the universal admiration of Travellers, situated thirty-eight degrees north latitude, on the East Bank of the Wabash, Navigable about 250 miles north, towards Lake Michigan." The property was suggested as suitable for "capitalists" or "large Religious Communities who may be desirous to form a settlement."[1]

Owen apparently had heard about the Rappite experiment some years earlier through a book written about the community. In 1820 he began a correspondence with the Reverend Mr. Rapp, eager to exchange his ideas of community life with someone who was undertaking a communal experiment in America. His first letter to Mr. Rapp read:

The Reverend Mr. Rapp.

Most worthy Sir: Having heard much of your Society, and feeling a peculiar interest respecting it, I am induced to open a correspondence with you, in the expectation of procuring a correct account of your establishment.

My first attention was called to it by some travels published in America by a Mr. Mellish, who in 1811 visited the original settlement near to Pittsburgh, and who gave many details which, to me, appeared to promise many future advantages. You have since had an opportunity of creating a second settlement, under the full benefit of the experience derived from the first, and the particulars of the result of these two experiments would be of real value to me, in order to ascertain the positive inconveniences which arise from changes to society from a state of private to public property, under the peculiar circumstances by which your colonies have been surrounded.

If you can furnish me with any authentic, printed or manuscript, statement of the rise, progress, and present state of Harmony, you would confer upon me a very particular obligation.

The gentleman who conveys this letter will perhaps have the goodness to take charge of them and bring them to England. Should this be inconvenient to him, any parcel addressed for me to New Lanark, North Britain, and forwarded to Mr. Quincy Adams, the Secretary of State for the American home department, would, I have no doubt, come safe.

There is a colony here of about 2400 persons, whom I have already placed under new circumstances, preparatory to a still more improved arrangement, from which incalculable advantages to all classes may be expected. I am now in the midst of preparing a further development of the system I have in view, and it will give me pleasure to send you a copy of it, the earliest opportunity after it shall be ready. In the mean time I send you copies of such works as I have already published, which I request you to accept. I am, sir, your most obedient

Robert Owen[2]

The following year Owen and a new partner, William Maclure, the Scottish geologist and founder of the Philadelphia Academy of

Natural Sciences who had visited and admired the New Lanark schools, purchased New Harmony for approximately $150,000.00. According to George Flower, the son of Richard Flower, the purchasing agent, New Harmony then consisted of several brick two-story houses, some three-story buildings, some log cabins, and George Rapp's large brick mansion. In addition there were gardens, a church, a granary, a water mill, an oil mill, shops of various trades with the appropriate tools, two orchards, two vineyards, and livestock.[3] At first a number of the Rappites remained in the community. Within a few months additional settlers arrived and soon the population of New Harmony exceeded by several hundreds the previous total of nine hundred residents. Owen gradually withdrew from his involvement in the New Lanark community, although its schools continued in operation on the Owen model until 1872, at which time they were integrated with the public school system established by the Scottish Education Act.

I A New Way of Life

Owen hoped to fulfill his ambitious plans in the United States where the land was less costly than in Europe and his experiments might attract the widest and most favorable attention among leading citizens everywhere. He was inspired by the same ideal that motivated the Puritans two centuries earlier when they had dreamed of their "City on a Hill" that would become a model of the proper way to live, a perfect society which all peoples could emulate. To Owen it seemed appropriate to begin such a society in a land of freedom and democracy. The new man would develop as the young country grew. He advised persons of influence in America to "manfully and promptly step forward, and place themselves in the gap between the present and the future, and . . . say to the world, 'Now shall the government of force, and fraud, and disunion cease, and from henceforth truth, and sincerity, and charity, and kindness, and union, shall take their place, and superstition and prejudice shall no longer have domination here!' "[4]

According to Owen, America, a land of "abundance of capacity to sustain and support, in high comfort, much more than all the present population of the old world"[5] was not utilizing its resources because, although political liberty existed here, "real mental liberty" did not. Owen planned to liberate America by means of introducing "into these States, and through them to the world at large, a new social system, formed in practice of an entire new combination of circumstances, all of them having a direct, moral, intellectual, and beneficial tendency, fully adequate to effect the most important improvements throughout society."[6] The principles governing his communities, he thought, were in complete harmony with the principles of the government of the United States. The United States was, therefore, to be the setting for the first step in a plan to remake the characters of the population of the world. What better place to begin anew than in a land unfettered by precedent, unhampered by aristocracy or monarchy, and unrestricted by rigid, centuries-old mental attitudes?

Owen's son William wrote in 1825 that the goal of New Harmony would be to achieve a community founded "on the Principle of united production and consumption, to be composed of persons practicing all the most useful occupations necessary to the well being of a complete establishment."[7] The residents would receive in return for their labor "lodgings, food, clothing, attendance during sickness and a good education for their children."[8] Note that education was to be a fundamental part of the scheme.

Robert Owen declared that his main purpose for transferring his activities to the United States was to display to the American people the means whereby they could achieve a more acceptable and more satisfying life style. He was convinced that the leaders in government needed only to be shown methods of improving the moral character of the masses, for it was certainly within the power of those leaders to decide "whether ignorance and poverty, and disunion, and counteraction, and deception, and imbecility, shall continue to inflict their miseries upon its [America's] subjects, or whether affluence, and intelligence, and union, and good feeling, and the most open sincerity, in all things, shall change the condition of this population, and give continually increasing prosperity to all the states, and secure happiness to every individual within them."[9]

Owen viewed New Harmony as a temporary haven, a step on the road to the new rational world. At New Harmony he expected the people to exemplify those habits necessary for the improvement of character and suitable to life in a world of brotherhood. Americans, he believed, would be flexible enough, owing to the relative newness of their institutions, to adapt themselves to his plans and fulfill his ideals. Where would it be more appropriate and promising to begin a new way of life than in the New World?

To Owen it seemed that the geographic location and physical characteristics of New Harmony made it perfectly suited to his experiments in this new way of life. One commentator wrote:

It is situated in a thickly wooded country, on the banks of the Wabash, on the Indiana side, at about thirty miles from the mouth of that river. The site of ground upon which the town stands, is generally flat for about a mile and a half from the river, when the surface of the country becomes hilly and pleasantly undulating. . . . The town is regularly laid out, in straight and spacious streets, crossing each other at right angles, in common with modern American towns. The log cabins are giving place as fast as possible to neat and commodious brick and framed houses, which are extremely well built, the uniform redness of the brick, of which the majority of them is composed, giving to the place a remarkable brightness of appearance. . . . The town is amply supplied with excellent wells, as also with public ovens, which are placed at regular and convenient distances from each other. The granaries, &c. are generally built in an exceedingly handsome and durable manner. There is also a pretty village church, the white steeple of which, seen from afar, through the widely extending clearings, and forests of girdled trees, seems to invite the traveller onward to a peaceful resting-place. [10]

The foregoing description of New Harmony by William Hebert, a British traveller in America, was written before Owen and Maclure purchased the village of 20,000 acres together with its houses, church, and mills, and makes it easy to understand the great attraction of the place for its future owners. Like Owen afterward, Hebert concluded that the success of a community in such a setting was assured: "No one indeed could doubt it [the success of the community] who had visited Harmony and seen the astonishing effects of the united and systematic industry of members, and the numerous comforts, as well as the security derived from this enlarged system of social intercourse." [11]

Another spectator, Captain Donald Macdonald, who journeyed with Owen to America in 1824, described the impact of suddenly

coming upon New Harmony after travelling for days through undeveloped land:

About 3000 acres of land is cleared around the village. In the background
lay the Wabash river about 100 yards wide, backed by the forest on its right
bank, & lost in the forests above & below the village. On the side of the
hills were the vineyards; & to the left of the road down to the village, lay
meadows, orchards and a neatly designed labyrinth. The village stood a
couple of hundred yards nearer to us than the river on rather a more
elevated bottom . . . . The ground on the right and between the village
& the hills was divided into corn fields. The village consisted of four streets
running towards the river, & six crossing these. In the middle was an open
space in which stood a wooden church with a steeple, and close to it a large
new brick church, which I afterwards learnt was built to replace the old one
which was not large enough. In various streets stood large & small brick
habitations, but the majority of houses were either log houses or small
wooden ones. At the back of the houses were gardens, all divided by
wooden palings. The village had a dark appearance, occasioned by un-
painted wood exposed to the air becoming of a dusky slate colour; but the
end bricks formed an agreeable contrast. To a traveller just emerging from
a forest where little or no improvement has taken place, and remembering
the many days he has spent in wandering through a thinly peopled & badly
cultivated country, the view from these hilly pastures down upon a rich
plain, flourishing village, and picturesque river winding through a magnifi-
cent forest, is highly gratifying.[12]

Besides the low cost of the land and the beauty of the setting,
several other attractions led Owen to conclude that Indiana would
be an ideal place for his experiment in a new way of life. Since the
area was sparsely settled and relatively undeveloped, the new
settlers were generally people of an adventuresome character willing and eager to face challenging situations. In contrast to the state
of affairs in Great Britain, there would be no taxes to burden the inhabitants, no military service or demands which could exhaust the
financial and human resources of the community. The sparsely pop-
ulated American West was not afflicted by the heavy hand of class
or race prejudice. Moreover, American newspapers had already
published favorable comments about Owen's work, and Owenite
societies had been formed in New York and Philadelphia. American
doors seemed wide open to welcome communal experiments in a
new way of life.

II   *Organization of the Community*

Since New Harmony was a functioning community when Owen and Maclure purchased it (just as New Lanark had been), the residents were familiar with their own ways and not particularly sympathetic to Owen's new ideas. Nevertheless, although quite a few left the community, some of the Rappites remained, chiefly for the sake of convenience and comfort. Owen did not immediately construct any master plan for changes, for he intended to meet specific problems one at a time as they arose. In April, 1825, however, he drew up a constitution for the settlement, stating therein that the goal of New Harmony was to promote the happiness of all residents, that an organization, The Preliminary Society of New Harmony, would be formed to set high ethical standards and improve the moral character of the members, that people of all ages and of any race would be welcome to become members, even though some might freely exercise their right to leave and join communities abroad. Some black members might eventually choose to settle in Africa. Owen as the proprietor would have the right to appoint members to the committee which was to manage the affairs of the community. Unusual provisions of the constitution required prospective members to agree that they would never act unkindly toward any other person, also that they would be "temperate, regular, and orderly"[13] as well as diligent in their work. All applicants for admission had to sign the constitution as an indication that they agreed to its terms.

No special policies or regulations concerning the property rights of members were promulgated. No specific qualifications for membership in the community were formulated, except that preference would be given to mature, experienced people. Eventually there were more applicants than could be accommodated. Each applicant was asked to provide the following information: name and age; age of spouse; number, ages, and sexes of children; place of birth; residence; occupation; and motive for wanting to join New Harmony. There was never more than a minimal screening of applicants, and during the first few weeks eight hundred people applied. Housing facilities soon became inadequate. Individuals differing widely in their financial circumstances simply migrated to New Harmony bringing whatever possessions they had and could transport, including money, furniture, and other personal effects. Those with substantial capital were received warmly and welcomed as nonworking members of the community, for there was no egalitarian policy. On the contrary, according to the Duke of Saxe-Weimar, who visited New Harmony, women of the upper classes had the advantage of being guided by a special teacher, a privilege not accorded to other women and, although the constitution stated that all members were to be treated as equals, some inequities developed.

New Harmony was organized as a typical Owenite agricultural and industrial community which would put into practice Owen's economic and social reforms. Workers were to receive credit toward goods necessary for their subsistence in proportion to the amount of labor they contributed. Most adults were required to perform services within their capacity; these were recorded in pass books issued to heads of families and to single persons; and goods were to be paid for on a quarterly basis, always one quarter in advance. Payment in cash was a rare occurrence. Wages in the form of credits were kept low enough so that workers would generally earn no more than they needed, and any surplus profits were not supposed to be accumulated by an individual or a small group but turned over to the whole community.

Owen had intended to supervise activities during his first year at New Harmony, but, as it turned out, he was more often than not absent from the community, leaving his sons, Robert Dale and William, in charge. In his absence matters were usually in "an unsettled state,"[14] and everyone waited impatiently for their benefactor's return. William Pelham, an enthusiastic resident during the Owenite experiment, conceded that during Owen's extended absences community affairs were often in a state of flux. "Want of organization and arrangement . . . caused much perplexity and difficulty."[15]

Since religious freedom was absolute, every resident could worship in accordance with his conscience or not at all if he so preferred. There were two churches in the community, one of which was put to secular uses, while the other was made available gratis to any minister who wished to preach in it. Consequently, services for various denominations were held, and one minister, a resident at New Harmony, delivered nondenominational sermons regularly, such as his sermon of August, 1825, "in plain language on how to receive religious impressions."[16] This policy of unrestricted religious freedom was maintained successfully despite complaints of pious critics against Owen because he had failed to provide for a uniform or systematic religious program, a criticism most probably attributable to Owen's reputation for indifference to religious matters rather than to the actual situation at New Harmony.

Early in 1826, when Owen returned to New Harmony from one of his frequent absences abroad, he was quite pleased with the progress the community had been making under the leadership of his sons, and therefore, two years sooner than he had planned to do so, he reorganized New Harmony into a Community of Equality, based on communal ownership of property, equality of rights, and equality of duties. In accordance with his revised constitution, the community was divided into six departments: agriculture, manufacturing, education, domestic economy, general economy, and commerce; each department was subdivided into occupations, and each of the latter was to be supervised by an Intendant.

This hastily devised new system necessitated numerous changes in the structure and affairs of the community. Legislative power was vested in an executive council and an assembly of all residents twenty-one years of age or older. Applicants for membership had to be approved by majority vote of the assembly. The system of wage payments in the form of merchandise doled out to each member in proportion to his work performance was eliminated, and henceforth each person was to receive whatever he needed but was expected to contribute his labor to the best of his ability. This honor system was applied to all community affairs with no provision to penalize the idle or dishonest members.

Unfortunately, these new arrangements imposed upon the residents greater responsibility than they were equipped to handle. Within a month's time, the community was in complete disarray. *The Western Luminary*, a Kentucky newspaper, reported in February, 1826, that "The establishment of Mr. Owen at Harmony is represented to be in a state of the utmost anarchy and confusion. Out of the entire population, amounting to 1150, it is reported that enough cannot be found to cut wood for the Society."[17] The executive committee appealed to Owen to resume his personal direction of affairs for one more year. As a staunch advocate of

democratic self-government, he had hoped to demonstrate its prac-
ticality in New Harmony, but it was apparent that the diversity of
personal backgrounds among the settlers had not prepared them for
such a venture requiring adjustment of their differences and full
cooperation in decisions. The new legislature lacked proper training
for its hastily assumed duties. As a result, early in 1826 the
membership split into competing factions and then divided into two
opposing communities: the first, called Macluria, was organized by
those who disagreed with Owen's views concerning religion; the second, called Feiba Peveli, was set up by members who accepted
Owen's views on religion and morality but agreed with residents of
Macluria about the best form of government for the community.
For some time Owen's presence and leadership kept the community
from total disruption, but its affairs remained unsettled, its future
course uncertain. Later in 1826, against his advice, the members
revised the constitution again, this time organizing themselves into
three societies (educational, agricultural, and mechanics and
manufacturing) and thereby making harmonious relationships virtually impossible. Disputes and lawsuits in the following year put an
end to Owen's experiment.

III   *Education*

Education at New Harmony was to be "the base upon which the
future prosperity and happiness of the community must be
founded." As such, it was to be the most important of the various
departments within the village. As he had at New Lanark, Owen set
out several principles on which the educational system was to be
based:

The children of the community shall be educated together, and as one
family, in the schools and exercise grounds provided for them in the centre
[sic] of the square; where they will at all times be under the eye and inspec-
tion of their parents.

By properly conducting their education, it will be easy to give each child
good tempers and habits; with as sound a constitution as air, exercise, and,
[sic] temperance, can bestow:

A facility in reading, writing, and accounts;

The elements of the most useful sciences, including geography and
natural history;

A practical knowledge of agriculture, and domestic economy, with a knowledge of some ONE [sic] useful manufacture, trade, or occupation, so that this employment may be varied, for the improvement of his mental and physical powers;

And lastly, a knowledge of himself and of human nature, to form him into a rational being, and render him charitable, kind, and benevolent, to all his fellow-creatures.[18]

The school at New Harmony (with an attendance of 130 pupils in 1825) duplicated the administrative organization that Owen had set up in New Lanark. He appointed Joseph Neef, a disciple of Pestalozzi, as director. Neef was an experienced teacher who had managed a school in the Philadelphia area for Maclure. Mme Neef, his wife, and another experienced teacher, Mme Marie Duclos Fretageot, took charge of educating the infants in the school. The staff were competent people who contributed innovative ideas to the school program.

One innovation far ahead of the times was the use of a rating scale to measure each pupil's abilities and progress. The scale was divided into five-point intervals from zero to one hundred points, enabling the teachers to rate every child's progress and keep him informed of his scores. Children received scores in such attributes as concentration of attention, affection, judgment, imagination, memory, reflection, perception, excitability, courage, and strength.[19] As in the case of Owen's silent monitor at New Lanark, this rating scale was designed as a stimulant of self-improvement, and it was hoped that it would result in better attitudes, desired behavior patterns, and greater efficiency in learning subject matter and skills.

Another innovation, one for which Maclure deserves credit, was the organization of an industrial department to provide training in taxidermy, printing, carpentry, dressmaking, cabinet-making, shoemaking, and other trades.

The teaching of science was given much more attention in New Harmony than had been the case at New Lanark, an emphasis also attributable to Maclure's initiative and interest. In 1826 many scientists and scholars arrived to join the community, so many, in fact, that their ship was referred to as the "Boatload of Knowledge," and thereafter New Harmony served as a meeting place for scientists from all parts of the world. Although numerous scholars settled in New Harmony owing to Maclure's influence, Owen's own reputation was sufficient to attract people of stature to the community: "Among the endless variety of people that flocked around Mr. Owen were some eminent in art, literature, and science. This gave to Harmony a pre-eminence in character and attractions to many neighboring towns."[20]

Life at New Harmony was highly structured, excessively so in the opinions of many residents, such as those who resented the tolling of bells to announce the time for meals or chores: the 5 o'clock bell to signal commencement of the day's business, the 7 o'clock breakfast gong, the 12 noon dinner bell, and the 6 o'clock supper bell. Breakfast for the children consisted of milk, molasses, and corn meal mush; dinner of meat and vegetables, and supper of mush and milk. School was often in session from 3 A.M. to 8 A.M. and from 1 P.M. to 3 P.M. During the remaining hours of the day the pupils worked at their trades. As at New Lanark, there were planned activities for evenings, such as dancing, musical performances, town meetings, and group discussions, but Monday and Saturday evenings the pupils were free to do whatever they preferred.

Children were kept in school, as Owen had wanted to do at New Lanark, until they were twelve years of age. Those whose families did not reside at New Harmony were accepted as boarders, paying an annual fee of $100 which covered education, board and room, clothing, and medicines. Children two years or older could be admitted as boarders. Older pupils, those twelve years or over, had the advantage of being taught by noted intellectuals, such as Thomas Say, the father of the science of descriptive entomology, and Charles Alexander Lesueur, the French naturalist and painter.

Owen's son, Robert Dale, while acting as supervisor of the school programs, forbade the use of corporal punishment for misbehavior. On the whole, however, the educational system, compared with the New Lanark schools, was more formalistic and rigid. For example, pupils walked from one assignment to another in rows and were allowed only fifteen minutes for breakfast. They were obviously not so carefree or happy as their counterparts in Scotland. When he was leaving New Harmony for good in 1827, Owen stated that the children had not been educated so as to develop correct behavior patterns, and he asserted that the Maclure faction had prevented implementation of his ideas on character formation. He complained that there had been excessive adherence to the Pestalozzian method of teaching, with its overemphasis upon the learning of subject matter so that the rounded development of each child had been largely neglected. But some of the educational deficiencies could be attributed to the fact that Owen himself devoted much less time to the New Harmony schools than he had given to the New Lanark schools. Moreover, at New Harmony he had concentrated his efforts on the over-all organization of the community rather than specific programs or departments. Owen's partner, Maclure, who was thus enabled to exert greater influence upon educational procedures, turning them in the direction of those Pestalozzian emphases which Owen deprecated, remained at New Harmony following Owen's departure and for a decade or more thereafter attempted without significant success to continue his educational experiments.

IV   *Failure of the Community*

Although Owen was generally well received in the United States by educators, politicians, and the press, it was not long before the community he had organized was subjected to considerable adverse criticism. Beginning at the time of his arrival in the country, he became an increasingly controversial figure as newspaper editors aligned themselves for or against him and his proposed reforms. A running debate ensued and persisted throughout his stay concerning the merits and defects of his system as practiced in New Harmony. In 1827 disruption of the community vindicated the judgment of those critics who had predicted that Owen's communal system would fail.

The failure of New Harmony must be attributed to basic short-comings rather than to specific disagreements among the directors. The frequent absence of Owen as leader of the community was an important factor, not necessarily due to his managerial skills, but rather because of the optimism and faith with which he inspired his adherents. Owen's personality seemed to provide the link between the theory and the reality of his communities. In addition, competent managers and skilled craftsmen were not attracted to the settlement in sufficient numbers, for they could receive greater prestige and higher compensation elsewhere without risking an uncertain future in a revolutionary experiment. Admission requirements for prospective settlers were too lax or vaguely defined, with the result that too many misfits, adventurers, idlers, and speculators were accepted who antagonized and interfered with the honest, hardworking adherents of Owen's goals and ideals. Some of the residents wished mainly to reap benefits from the labor of others. The large, diverse population made Owen's cooperative plans and policies most difficult to implement. Even housing conditions, so important for the health and happiness of the people, deteriorated. The honor system of wage payments for labor proved to be unsatisfactory, a situation compounded by an unnecessarily complicated bookkeeping apparatus. Family disputes often resulted in broken marriages, inasmuch as community regulations made it easy to dissolve them. Most importantly, the adoption of one new constitution after another confused the people, who could not adjust to the everchanging rules, and separated them into competing factions, of which in 1828 there were as many as ten representing a great variety of views.

Internally, New Harmony never achieved that equality among its members which its benefactor envisioned. According to Thomas Pears and his wife Sarah, residents during its first year of operation, many were unwilling to sacrifice personal comforts for the good of the community or even to perform the chores assigned to them. For this reason Sarah Pears felt that instead of doing work in the kitchen, she "would rather, far rather, that Mr. Owen would shoot me through the head."[21] She considered it cruel to take young children away from their families and called the schools "shameful." According to Mrs. Pears, "The boys have learnt nothing, and the girls have learnt a little geography, and a little sewing, but plenty of bad langauge, disobedience and contempt for their teachers."[22] She commented that the situation was intolerable for most of the residents, since they had come to New Harmony for the sake of the proper education of their children. She herself expressed resentment at having to work alongside "rough uncouth creatures . . . hard to look upon . . . in the light of brothers and sisters."[23] In May, 1826, sorely disappointed, the Pears gave up their membership and left the community.

Robert Dale Owen suggested that the settlement might have endured if no drastic social reforms had been undertaken, that workers in the United States did not need the kind of protective arrangements that had been useful to them in Great Britain. But the breakup of the community did not occur over disagreements concerning such matters as working conditions or compensation. Disputes between Owen and Maclure about the system of education and the financial policies of the community brought matters to a head early in 1827.

Maclure came to view Owen's theories of education and communal living as unrealistic and his personality as abrasive. But earlier, in 1824, on learning that Owen planned to establish a community in the United States, Maclure could hardly contain his enthusiasm:

Mr. Robert Owen of New Lanark is now here and intends making the United States the theatre of his future experiments on the facility of rendering the human species happy, and proving the infinite satisfaction, pleasure and happiness derived from the attempt of such a self approbating work. Nothing on earth can give more satisfaction and pleasure than the certainty of the only man in Europe who has a proper idea of mankind and the use he ought to make of his faculties is going to join the finest and most rational Society on the Globe.[24]

By 1826, however, Maclure had become disillusioned with Owen's schemes, and impatient with his partner. He came to see Owen more and more as a dreamer of dreams, not as an architect of a new society. Owen's communities were, Maclure said, based on "wild theories." His personality was "most obstinate in action" and his character was "most vain."[25] Maclure even attacked Owen's theories of education, which so recently had won his praises: "He [Owen] has not the smallest idea of a good education and will not permit any to flourish within his reach. His parot [sic] education to exhibit before strangers as at New Lanark is the whole he knows."[26] Maclure by this time thought it utterly impossible that Owen would ever realize his schemes for changing "the confirmed habits of adults in 10 times the length of time his enthusiasm allots for it."[27]

Maclure held that it would be futile to attempt to reeducate adults, whereas Owen was convinced that such a program was not only possible but essential both to the education of children and to the achievement of social reforms. Maclure favored permanent classes to each of which one teacher would be assigned who could become familiar with the needs and progress of the individual child from one year to the next. Owen opposed such a procedure, declaring the kind of education a child thus received would depend upon the ability of only a single teacher and would be different from that of other children in the school. In practice, the teachers did not conform to either of these points of view but shifted from one to the other so that, for example, teachers assigned to teach infants could be found actually teaching children of all ages. Eventually the school split into two systems, one managed by Owen's assistant, the other by Maclure.

A heated quarrel between the two partners, involving them in lawsuits and countersuits, ended their partnership in 1827; in the summer of that year Owen began to sell his share of the land at great personal loss and returned to England an impoverished man. In 1828 Owen offered his explanation for the failure of New Harmony:

I came here with a determination to try what could be effected in this new country to relieve my fellowmen from superstition and mental degradation; so that, if successful, the experiment should be an example which all might follow and by which all might benefit.

I tried here a new course for which I was induced to hope that fifty years of political liberty had prepared the American population: that is, to govern themselves advantageously. I supplied land, houses, and the use of much capital; and I tried, each in their own way, all the different parties who collected here; but experience proved that the attempt was premature to unite a number of strangers not previously educated for the purpose, who should carry on extensive operations for their common interest and live together as a common family.

However, in his optimistic way, Owen reasserted his plans for social reform. The failure of the people at New Harmony to adapt to preferable modes of behavior indicated to Owen an even greater need to carry on his policies and experiments. He continued,

But is the population of the world to be left in this miserable and hopeless state? If *all* we desire cannot be effected for this generation, so as to produce honesty, industry, intelligence, independence and happiness, by reason of the habits and feelings that have arisen out of their superstitious training; ought we to abandon them and their offspring to their errors and miseries? Ought we not rather to redouble our exertions to stop the evil from proceeding any farther and never be weary in well doing? If we cannot do all now, let us do whatever is practicable; and make as great an advance towards the right road as we can make with the means we possess.[28]

Despite the failure of the experiment, only two years after its inception, New Harmony made several lasting contributions to social and educational reform. As George Flower pointed out, many of Owen's most enduring reforms were not achieved until after he had left New Harmony: "The halls of legislation, the courts of law, and the family government have been modified and influenced by the opinions promulgated by Mr. Robert Owen in the early days of his Harmony community, followed up by the after-efforts of his son, Mr. Robert Dale Owen, in the State legislature."[29]

Owen was a pioneering advocate of equality for the sexes. Women in the community had the right to vote in the assembly and shared with the men equally in the ownership of the communal property. The school was perhaps the first in the United States to provide identical education to girls and boys. Free, universal education was put into effect. Many years before 1860, when Elizabeth P. Peabody opened a kindergarten in Boston, Owen established the first infant school in the United States, the kirst kindergarten in the Western Hemisphere, the first kindergarten as part of a public school system, as well as libraries, literary societies, and thespian societies, while he and his partner organized the second industrial school in the nation and helped pave the way for many Pestalozzian methods of education in the country. The experiment at New Harmony highlighted the need of people everywhere for social and educational reforms, the difficulties and pitfalls to be avoided in future experiments, and Owen's pioneering theories of education.

V   The Owen Legacy

Robert Owen and Anne Caroline Dale Owen had eight children. Those who lived beyond early adulthood moved to New Harmony and contributed much to the development of nineteenth-century America. Arthur H. Estabrook, who traced the genealogy of the Owen family, said that Owen's wife was descended from a line of English and Scottish noblemen. He traced Mrs. Owen's heritage back to "all the English Kings back of Edward III and all the French Kings back of Philip le bel."[30] Estabrook attributed qualities such as altruism, charm, graciousness, musical and artistic talent, gentleness, and kindness to the Owen family. Examining the lives of Owen's descendants, Estabrook discovered that "a high grade of intellectual abilty is found in Robert Owen and his three genius sons [Robert Dale Owen, David Dale Owen, and Richard Dale Owen] . . . . It is interesting to add here that not a single feeble-minded person is found in the Owen family."[31] Estabrook concluded that "the fact that three of his [Owen's] sons became very prominent in the development of this country makes the Owen family one of interest to students of genealogy, biography, eugenics and heredity."[32]

Robert Dale Owen, as did others of the Owen children, adopted his father's projects and served to publicize and expound his theories. Far from being pressured as progeny of a famous father, the Owen children seemed to thrive on his energies. In 1824 Robert Dale Owen dedicated his first publication to his father:

I dedicate this my first production to you, my dear Father, because I trace the formation of a great part of my own character, and the origin of a great part of my own feelings and sentiments to yourself.

In teaching me to think, you led me to examine principles, intimately connected with the best interests of mankind; and I feel that I have derived both pleasure and profit from the examination.[33]

Robert Dale Owen (1801 - 1877), the oldest son, was perhaps the most renowned of the Owen children. He was a statesman, publicist, editor, author, and legislator. He served three terms in the Indiana legislature (1836 - 38), during which time he secured funds for public schools. He was elected to the United States House of Representatives in 1842 as a Democrat, and later appointed minister to Naples. He supported the annexation of Texas and advocated a firm position in the Oregon boundary dispute. He presented his view of the inequities of slavery to Lincoln, and at the end of the Civil War was chairman of a committee to investigate the conditions of freedmen. He supported the work of Susan B. Anthony, advocating women's rights and freedom in divorce, and served as vice-president of the Indiana Women's Suffrage Association. He was successful in securing independent property rights for married women and widows in Indiana. He helped to organize the Smithsonian Institution and was a member of its first board of regents.

As an author, Robert Dale Owen was prolific. He did not confine himself to any one topic, but wrote on a wide range of interests. Some of his better-known publications include *An Outline of The System of Education at New Lanark* (1824), *Footfalls on the Boundary of Another World* (1859), *The Wrong of Slavery, the Right of Emancipation, and the Future of the African Race in the United States* (1864), *Debatable Land between this World and the Next* (1872), and the autobiography of his first twenty-seven years, *Threading My Way* (1874). Moreover, he served as co-editor with his father of some Owenite journals. In 1832 Robert Dale Owen married Mary Jane Robinson, the daughter of a Puritan from Connecticut and Virginia. The wedding was much publicized because the famous groom and his bride wrote their own marriage contract. After her death he married Lottie Walton Kellogg (in 1876). Robert Dale Owen died in 1877. He had, during some fifty years in America, served his adopted country well.

Richard Dale Owen (1810 - 1890) and David Dale Owen (1807 - 1860) were instrumental in the development of geological research in the United States, and both became professors in American colleges. David graduated from the Ohio Medical College at Cincinnati in 1836, but soon turned to geology as his major interest. A well-known geologist and draftsman, David became the state geologist of Indiana. In 1837 he conducted a preliminary geological survey of Indiana. In 1839 he was appointed geologist of the United States. Richard succeeded his brother as the state geologist of Indiana. In 1849 Richard became a professor of natural science at the Western Military Institute of Kentucky. In 1864 he held the chair of natural science at the Indiana State University. During the Civil War he served as a colonel in the Indiana infantry. Both Richard and David maried daughters of Joseph Neef, a teacher at New Harmony.

Anne Caroline Owen died in London in 1830. Anne, Owen's eldest daughter, had been a teacher in the New Lanark schools. Mrs. Owen, wife of Robert Owen, died in 1831, followed by the death of another daughter, Mary, in 1832. After the deaths of her mother and sisters, Jane Dale Owen (1805 - 1861) joined her brothers at New Harmony where she met and married Robert Henry Fauntleroy, who was a geologist with the United States Coast Survey as well as an astronomer and a meteorologist. Jane's daughter, Constance Fauntleroy, founded the first women's club in America, the Minerva Club, at New Harmony in 1858.

William Owen (1802 - 1841) settled at New Harmony, too, and was co-editor of the *New Harmony Gazette* along with Robert Dale Owen and other residents of the community. While Robert Owen travelled, William, apparently the most business-minded son, often supervised business affairs at New Harmony. William, the founder of the Thespian Society, married Mary Bolton, the daughter of a resident during the experiment at New Harmony.

Because of the large degree of success the Owen children a-chieved in their careers, the stress Owen put on academic ac-complishments and independent responsibility must have made the adjustment to adult life easy for his family. How much of their success is directly attributable to environmental factors in their up-bringing and how much to the privileged position the Owens en-joyed in society and to innate ability and ambition cannot be measured. Owen was, however, justifiably proud of his children. They, in turn, were fond of and grateful to their father, and gave him financial aid in his time of need, after the failure of his experi-ment at New Harmony.

Mrs. David Dale Owen expressed the pride of the Owen family in a remark about New Harmony made to her granddaughter: "Other towns . . . were founded for gain or because the people were un-successful at home, but ours was founded for an ideal—for the good of humanity."[34]

Partly because the family had continued to live in New Harmony for so many decades after dissolution of the utopian settlement, as did many of the teachers and scientists the community had at-tracted, the town retained its wide reputation as a center of culture and learning.

By the end of the nineteenth century, however, intellectual life in New Harmony had stagnated. Today, some one hundred and fifty years after Robert Owen's departure from Indiana, the reconstruc-tion and preservation of New Harmony is underway. Mrs. Jane Blaffer Owen, the wife of Kenneth Dale Owen, a geologist—aided by the state, private philanthropists, and foundations—originated the idea of a massive renovation. With her encouragement, a revival of academic and cultural activity is currently taking place in New Harmony.

CHAPTER 11

Owen's Influence during his Lifetime

THE influence of Robert Owen's views and practical experiments spread widely in Western countries during his lifetime and has continued to affect social and educational reform movements to this day. Mention has been made of his contributions to the advance of socialism, which has undoubtedly inspired reforms in nonsocialist countries as well, and his innovations in education which have been practiced in national school systems throughout the world. His influence upon institutions of his own time was dramatic and highly productive of results, including the formation of many Owenite communities in the United States and Europe, the publication of Owenite journals, the organization of Owenite societies, and the impact of his ideas upon visitors to New Lanark and upon world leaders.

I Owenite Communites in the United States

Frequently Robert Owen appealed to the public in behalf of his socialistic ideals, stressing that their implementation would remake human nature and create communities far superior morally, culturally, and materially than any which had ever existed under competitive arrangements of society. He never tired of reiterating his faith in cooperation as a way of life:

It will be readily admitted, that a population trained in regular habits of temperance, industry, and sobriety; of genuine charity for the opinions of all mankind, founded on the only knowledge that can implant true charity in the breast of any human being; trained also in a sincere desire to do good to the utmost of their power, and without any exception, to every one of their fellow-creatures, cannot, even by their example alone, do otherwise than materially increase the welfare and advantages of the neighbourhood in which such a population may be situated.[1]

He awakened the conscience of multitudes, especially leading personalities who agreed with his conclusion that well-managed communities of a new type could usher in an era of good feeling, high morality, and happiness among all peoples, and the result was that many cooperative communities sprung up throughout the Western world, including a number of remarkable experiments in the United States.[2]

Frances (Fanny) Wright (1795 - 1852), lecturer, defender of women's rights and suffrage, advocate of free public education, and abolitionist, founded Nashoba, a cooperative community of blacks in Tennessee. It was her idea that slaves could earn wages while at the same time acquiring the attitudes and skills necessary for wise use of their freedom, an objective similar to Owen's aim of improving the condition of the poor. Although the community, organized in 1825 with an initial membership of fifteen blacks, became interracial because of the theory that integrated education would establish racial equality, the white members admitted actually managed the affairs of the society in paternalistic fashion. Robert Dale Owen, who took a personal interest in Nashoba, visited Miss Wright and corresponded with her concerning its problems. The community was viewed with suspicion by its neighbors owing to the founder's attacks on religion, unorthodox views about birth control and the marriage contract, and radical ideas regarding race relations and the equalization of wealth. During her illness in 1828, the members gave up their short-lived experiment and disbanded. Miss Wright then became a resident of New Harmony where she met M. Phiquepal D'Arusmont, a teacher, whom she married in 1838.

Another cooperative community, the Franklin Community of New York State, formed in 1826, adopted one of the constitutions that Owen had prepared for New Harmony, including some of his most radical proposals. After only five months in operation, the community dissolved because of mounting financial difficulties and spirited disputes over the secularization of the schools and the creation of a Church of Reason. Some of the residents did not clearly understand Owenite precepts and reforms. One prominent, dissatisfied member complained against excessive permissiveness, too much freedom of speech, the omission of religious dogmas in the school, and atheism in the community; regretted that books were not given to children under twelve; and charged that the directors, not the majority of members, were managing the entire enterprise.[3] Before resigning, he admitted that he had not known the principles of the community when he joined and could no longer endure them. The main cause of the early failure of this community appears to have been the lack of essential programs (always recommended by Robert Owen) of training and moral reeducation to prepare the residents to undertake visionary reforms.

Also founded in 1826 was the rather more successful Kendal Community of Ohio. In order to avert initial financial difficulties confronting many cooperative communities, in the beginning each family invested sufficient funds of its own to purchase a portion of the land. Moreover, the members were local people well known to one another as persons worthy of trust. Nevertheless, financial problems developed and excessive debts accumulated until, in 1829, the community was amicably disbanded.

A similar fate attended the Coal Creek Community and Church of God enterprise in Indiana which ended in 1832 following the resignation of a former leader of the Shakers, William Ludlow, who had founded the community eight years previously but could no longer cope with ever-increasing financial and administrative difficulties. This settlement, located 150 miles from New Harmony, had prospered under Ludlow's idealistic leadership, but decline ensued as more and more of the participants displayed lack of understanding of Owenite doctrines or put their own short-term selfish interests above those of the community. Owen himself had realized the adverse effects stemming from lack of understanding and of dedication among the rank and file, and for this reason had emphasized the need for basic reeducation of the members in cooperative communities. Among the American communities a period of prosperity achieved through enthusiastic work of members and idealistic leadership could not be sustained in the absence of effective programs of adult education. Some of Owen's schemes, such as his proposal in 1828 to colonize Coahuila and Texas, then a province of Mexico, were never carried out, owing to financial problems or to religious or governmental influences. Several of the communities, like the Community of Yellow Springs, Ohio, organized in 1825 by a Swedenborgian minister (with an initial membership of one hundred) and the Franklin Community of New York State, collapsed within a few months of financial difficulties, while a few others such as the Nashoba, Kendal, and Coal Creek and Church of God experiments lasted a few years. Owen's advocacy of socialistic settlements, however, had a major impact upon the working class, reflected in their repeated futile attempts to organize these types of communities and in new attitudes of the masses who turned to other, more successful forms of cooperative living, as in cooperative societies, labor organizations, and other institutions or programs to protect their interests.

II *Owenite Communities in Great Britain*

Of the numerous Owenite communities organized in Great Britain early in the nineteenth century, the best known, in addition to New Lanark, were the Orbiston, Ralahine, and Queenwood communities.

Orbiston was founded in 1825 by Abram Combe, a prosperous Edinburgh manufacturer who had visited New Lanark in 1820 and had promptly become a convert to Owenism. To establish the settlement he purchased 290 acres of land at the site located near Glasgow and later contributed substantial sums to assist the residents.

A building four stories high was erected at Orbiston to serve as the central headquarters of the community, spacious enough to accommodate three hundred people. Here there were shared kitchens and lounges for all, although each adult had a private bedroom. The children, as at New Harmony which was in operation at the same time, lived in dormitories, separated from their parents. Combe advanced the funds needed for the education and living costs of each child, but this arrangement was on a loan basis and the debt was to be repaid by the child upon reaching maturity. Meanwhile, the educational program was integrated with employment comparable to modern work-study plans so that the children could earn enough to pay part of the costs of room, board, and schooling. The staff of teachers consisted of two teachers of academic subjects and practical skills and one dance instructor. The community published its own journal, *The Orbiston Register*.

At first Combe did not follow Owen's example of active leadership in the community, but preferred to observe the residents without interference, for he felt that people should be free to make their own decisions and solve their own problems. But the administration of affairs became so loose that no specific tasks were assigned to qualified persons, work in the kitchens and on the farm was neglected, and bickering among the members increased to such an extent that by the summer of 1826 Combe was compelled to take charge of many activities. He apportioned household tasks among the women, organized an iron foundry, a dairy company, a group of weavers, and another of shoemakers. Unfortunately Combe died in August of 1827 at a time when the community appeared to have achieved high efficiency and success in its undertakings. The tragic loss of their leader, coupled with a heavy burden of debt, made it impossible for the members to continue the experiment in communal living. In the fall of 1827 Orbiston, which had become one of the most renowned of the Owenite communities, ended its brief career in tragic failure. The buildings were dismantled. Combe's family was left destitute, and in the same year Owen himself was impoverished by the failure of New Harmony.

A number of Owenite communities were established in Ireland, of which Ralahine, an agricultural community in County Clare, was outstanding. This community was founded in 1831 by John Scott Vandeleur, a wealthy aristocrat who owned the land, and E. T. Craig, the Corresponding Secretary of the Manchester Owenian Society. Craig organized the community school, in which he himself served as teacher of older children and adults. A young woman taught the younger children until she married outside the community, whereupon she was asked to leave. The older children were well supplied with books, globes, and other learning aids. For the infants there was a playground equipped with ropes and swings. The curriculum included customary academic subjects but omitted religion. Physical exercises were prescribed for all children. As at New Lanark and New Harmony, three evenings weekly were given over to dancing, music, and lectures. Owen maintained close contacts with the Ralahine community, noting that the residents, though not all of them were convinced Owenites, accepted his basic principles and methods. The community seems to have functioned successfully until 1833, at which time Vandeleur gambled his fortune away in Dublin and lost his equity in Ralahine. Unable to pay his debts, he fled to England, and the residents of the community were dispossessed.

During the 1830s, far from becoming discouraged by the failures of numerous predecessors, many enthusiastic adherents of Owenism organized new cooperative communities in England. One of the best known was the Queenwood community established in 1839 by the Universal Community Society of Rational Religionists of which Owen was President until 1842. In this Hampshire community named Harmony Hall, a Quaker teacher was put in charge of the children, and an entire floor of the building was reserved for school use by the ninety-four pupils in attendance. As had been the case at New Harmony, the curriculum at Harmony Hall combined vocational training with academic subjects. The community owned 533 acres of land in Queenwood, but this proved to be a disadvantage, for the managers accepted too many applicants for residence and invested excessively in the construction of buildings requiring for their completion capital expenditures which the members were unable to provide or obtain. Moreover, there were not enough experienced farmhands to cultivate the land, nor enough horses and cows, nor enough tools with which to do the work. In 1844, after six years of participation in cooperative projects, including a fairly successful school program, the familiar problems of inept management, financial deficits, and spreading discontent among the members inevitably led to the termination of the community.

III   *Owenite Journals and Societies*

Robert Owen's influence spread widely in Great Britain through the journals and societies disseminating his views. Some of the journals were independent publications of Owenites, while others were organs of the societies.

Among the former the most effective were *The Crisis; or, the Change from Error and Misery, to Truth and Happiness*, and *Robert Owen's Journal*, published 1850 - 1852, which indicated its aims in a subtitle: *Explanatory of the Means to Well-Place, and Well-feed, Well-Clothe, Well-Lodge, Well-Employ, Well-Educate, Well-Govern, and Cordially Unite, the Population of the World. The Crisis*, edited by Robert Owen and Robert Dale Owen, stated its aims as being to halt the working classes from sinking further into "poverty, crime, and wretchedness" and to promote "Truth and happiness—by Education and Employment, the only possible mode by which such results can ever be produced."[4] *Robert Owen's Journal* was preceded by another journal, *The Economist*, published during 1821 - 1822, which similarly expounded and advocated Owen's proposed system of society. Among the best-known journals of societies were *The Co-operative Magazine and Monthly Herald*, published from 1826 to 1830 by the London Co-operative and Economical Society, and the journal of the Brighton Co-operative Benevolent Fund Association, which in 1830 had three hundred branch societies in the British Isles. There were numerous journals of both kinds advocating Owen's social reforms and cooperative communities, but, like the Owenite communities themselves, most of them were short-lived for the same reasons of poor management and lack of funds.

Only one of the Owenite societies was for a few years successful in establishing an Owenite community, namely, the aforementioned community at Queenwood founded by the Universal Community Society of Rational Religionists. But other societies contributed in some way to the advancement of Owen's educational, philanthropic, communitarian, or socialistic theories and programs. The Practical Society of Edinburgh, founded in 1821, operated not only a cooperative store but also a school along Owenite lines for as many as five hundred families. The London Co-operative and Economical Society attempted to make converts to Owen's views by means of lectures, discussions and debates, journals, and social breakfasts, and for years persisted, without success, in efforts to raise enough money to establish Owenite villages. The British and Foreign Philanthropic Society, established in 1822 on the initiative of Robert Owen, though unable to organize cooperative communities, sponsored a variety of measures in behalf of the working class, using especially the techniques (reeducation, employment, morale-building, and social emulation) that had been utilized successfully at New Lanark. The Brighton Co-operative Benevolent Fund Association was also successful in disseminating information about Owen's ideas among its numerous branches and in operating an Owenite school.

IV   *Labor Exchanges*

In 1832 Owen opened the National Equitable Labour Exchange in London. At the Exchange workers were to trade their goods for labor notes, which would entitle them to purchase merchandise. The purposes of the Exchange were to eliminate shopkeepers and to make quality goods available to workers on an exchange basis. "The producer deposits what he wishes to dispose of; the consumer selects what he desires to obtain. The price that is fair between the two is estimated by a disinterested committee of valuers. The total expense on the transaction is eight and a third per cent. The producer receives at once the representative of his labor, which representative will obtain for him an equal value in any of the other Bazaar stores."[5]

Owen had long thought money to be "the root, if not of *all evil*, of great injustice, oppression and misery to the human race, making some slavish producers of wealth, and others its wasteful consumers or destroyers."[6] The proceeds of labor, Owen asserted, rightfully belonged to the producers of labor, but rarely did they control it. Therefore, Owen considered this system of exchange to be far superior for several reasons to the more usual system of paying money for goods:

First, the producer can, under the old plan, obtain no representatives of his labor until he actually exchanges or sells it. Secondly, he has little or no opportunity of coming into contact with those who would exchange with him. Thirdly, he usually pays from 20 to 200 per cent. in addition to the original prime cost. Fourthly, he cannot ascertain what that per centage is, be it more or less. Fifth, he has no rational ground for confidence, that the price asked is the fair value of the article.[7]

Owen had great plans for the labor exchanges. He envisioned a system of exchanges with branches in various cities. In fact, several branches did open. Owen expected the exchanges to effect a redistribution of wealth in favor of the producing classes. "Equitable Labour Exchanges will increase wealth, of which labour is the source. They will make those who are now artificially poor, rich, and those who are artificially rich, poor . . . . Unfettered by money, real wealth will increase, poverty disappear, and crime proportionally diminish; and what education with all its precepts, — eloquence with all its blandishments, — law with all its severity, — and religion with all its sanctity, have not been able to effect, Equitable Labour Exchanges will ultimately accomplish."[8]

Initially the labor exchanges achieved a measure of prosperity.

Owen's National Equitable Labour Exchange in London during an eight-week period in September and October of 1833 handled 376,-166 exchanges. Business, therefore, was estimated to be equal to £50,000 per annum.[9] However, success was short-lived. Workers did not become independent as Owen had predicted; nor did paupers cease to exist. By 1834, due to inefficient management, pilferage, and disputes with the property owner, the National Equitable Labour Exchange was in debt and therefore forced to close its doors.

The efforts of all such journals and societies during the 1820s and thereafter shifted the Owenite movement in Great Britain so that it became not merely a tool of philanthropists but a practical instrument of social reform in the hands of the working classes, who were interested in cooperation primarily as a means of obtaining a good share of the profits of the new industrial system. Workers wanted to make immediate economic gains by organizing cooperative retail stores as consumers and trade unions as employees. Owen himself, generally sympathetic to ambitions of the workers, did not approve of cooperative stores, but he did encourage strongly the formation of trade unions. After most of the cooperative communities failed, however, a new type of cooperative retailing, wholesaling, producing, and distributing goods developed, beginning in 1844 with the Rochdale cooperative of twenty-eight men in England, and by 1889 the membership in such cooperatives had grown to exceed 800,000 families. Thus out of Owen's agitation for cooperative efforts to achieve economic and social reform have evolved the enormous cooperative enterprises of Great Britain, the Scandinavian countries, the United States, India, and other lands.

V *Contemporary Reactions*

Owen's ideas had a significant influence upon community leaders and prominent figures whose reactions were most often favorable but sometimes negative as in the case of the clergy who were offended by his view of religions as "geographic insanities" and his opposition to the teaching of religious dogmas. Unqualified praise came from thousands of visitors to New Lanark, including many notables, some of whom began to consider the possibility of following his example. Grand Duke Nicholas of Russia was so greatly impressed with what he saw at New Lanark that he offered to adopt Owen's two youngest sons and invited large numbers of people to leave England and settle in Russia in order to establish Owenite cooperative communities on land that he would donate for this purpose. According to Robert Dale Owen, nearly twenty thousand people signed the visitors' book at New Lanark during the period 1815 to 1825,[10] and Robert Owen stated that among the thousands who came annually to observe the school programs were Princes John and Maximilian of Austria, the Grand Duchess of Oldenburgh (later Queen of Würtemberg), and "Foreign Ambassadors, many bishops, and clergy innumerable—almost all our own nobility,—learned men of all professions from all countries,—and wealthy travellers for pleasure or knowledge of every description."[11]

What the visitors to New Lanark found, according to Owen, was a well-regulated society composed of members of the least fortunate classes living in most enviable circumstances.

They saw a population that had been indolent, dirty, imbecile, and demoralized, to a lamentable extent, who had become actively industrious, cleanly, temperate, and very generally moral, in all their proceedings. They saw the children of these people trained and educated, from two years of age and upwards, without individual reward or punishment, and they had never seen children who were their equals, in disposition, habits, manners, intelligence, and kind feelings, or who appeared to enjoy an equal degree of active happiness.[12]

The reactions of visitors were almost always enthusiastic. In 1819 a committee which was organized under the chairmanship of the Duke of Kent to investigate Owen's aims and accomplishments reported that

The population was found to be actively industrious, temperate, moral, well satisfied with their condition, and in the possession of more substantial advantages than any other population they had seen.

But the benefit the children of these people derived from the arrangements which have been made for their early training and subsequent education was of the most peculiar and valuable description, and must be seen to be understood.

The parties [visitors] state that the happiness of these children, even from three years of age, exceeds everything of the kind they ever witnessed; and that their conduct in all respects was equal to their happiness.[13]

One admiring visitor to New Lanark was Professor Pictet, the famous Swiss scholar and former Commissioner of Education in France, who persuaded Owen to accompany him on a tour of Europe, during which Pictet introduced him to some of the leading personalities of the Continent. On that tour Owen visited Father Jean Frédéric Oberlin's pioneering infant school for the poor in northeastern France, Pestalozzi's Institute at Yverdon, and Fellenberg's industrial school at Hofwyl. It would be impossible to estimate with confidence how many visitors to New Lanark may have been impelled by Owen's example to initiate similar experiments. Maclure, who later became Owen's partner at New Harmony, declared: "I never saw so many men, women and children with happy & contented countenances, nor so orderly, cheerfull & sober a society without any coertion or physical restraint."[14] Maclure stated that the success at New Lanark despite opposition from both church and state gave him the courage he needed to organize a similar farm and school of his own.

Reactions to Owen's writings reflected the profound influence of his ideas. His first four essays on the formation of character in his *A New View of Society* were published in five large editions in England and were translated into French and German. According to Owen, "all the leading and most respectable publishers were desirous of having their names to the work."[15] John Quincy Adams, American ambassador to London in 1816, requested copies for distribution to the President and Cabinet and to the governors of all the states. Owen convinced the British government that they ought to send copies to monarchs and prime ministers of every European country. Owen stated that even Napoleon, then in exile on Elba, received and reacted favorably to the essays.

In the United States Owen enjoyed fruitful discussions with leading statesmen, including John Adams, Thomas Jefferson, James Madison, James Monroe, Andrew Jackson, Henry Clay, John C. Calhoun, and Martin van Buren, and also with the most distinguished educators, journalists, and other intellectuals, many of whom were profoundly impressed with his views. In Europe he promoted his ideas effectively in meetings with influential leaders, as for example, Prince Metternich (who is said to have put some of Owen's ideas into practice), the King of Prussia (who established a national system of education based on Owen's principles), and the

Duke of Kent, father of the infant Queen Victoria, (who supported Owen's proposals and at one time headed a group of notables including the Duke of Sussex, Sir Robert Peel, and various members of Parliament) who attempted unsuccessfully to raise large sums with which to organize Owenite communities. Owen was called as an expert witness when Parliament investigated the status of education in Great Britain.

It is significant that in both Great Britain and the United States Owen was given extensive press coverage. In 1817, the year Owen presented his plans to alleviate the condition of the poor by establishing cooperative communities, Owen's lectures, letters, and sketches and diagrams of his proposed villages were often given as much as a full page in *The Times* (London). At that time *The Times* consisted of only four pages, at least one of which was devoted to commercial advertisements. Letters from readers commenting on Owen's plans as well as editorials about Owen were often to be found in *The Times*. Even though the editors were not necessarily in agreement with Owen's ideas, they did consider his writings to be of interest and importance to their readers, and so influential that the omission of a report on Owen's activities might be interpreted as an indication of opposition to his plans.[16]

Similarly, in 1825 the American newspapers abounded with reports of Owen's speeches to Congress. Some journals even reprinted his speeches in full. Apparently, Owen's arrival in America competed with the inauguration of President John Quincy Adams as the most newsworthy event of the season.

Owen was a prolific writer and a tireless lecturer. All who listened to him, whether or not in agreement with his theories or persuaded by his arguments, were moved by his enthusiasm, intensity, sincerity, gentle manner, and charm. Mrs. Frances Trollope who attended some of his lectures described his style of oratory thus:

The gentle tone of his voice; his mild, sometimes playful, but never ironical manner; the absence of every vehement or harsh expression; the affectionate interest expressed for 'the whole human family;' the air of candour with which he expressed his wish to be convinced he was wrong, if he indeed were so — his kind smile — the mild expression of his eyes — in short, his whole manner, disarmed zeal, and produced a degree of tolerance that those who did not hear him would hardly believe possible.[17]

Not even those who opposed Owen could doubt his sincerity; nor did they often get the better of him in a debate. Owen, who seemed to regard debate as a sport, developed his technique of arguing so that he confused his opponents, and wore them down as he held steadfastly to his main points. The best they could hope for would be a draw.

Mr. Owen, who was very powerful in colloquy, seldom lost an opportunity of explaining, what was then called, his new system of society. Discussion would arise; his system, doctrines, and their probable consequences were all discussed, fully criticised, and often warmly opposed. Mr. Owen possessed so steady a temper, that no attack, however violent and personal, could disturb it. The equanimity of his deportment, the quiet flow of argument, the steady and unaltered tone of his voice, I never knew to be ruffled by the most violent language and the sometimes hasty imputations of his opponent.[18]

Among the most prominent social reformers and educators whose reactions attested to the influence of Robert Owen were Lord Henry Peter Brougham, Samuel Wilderspin, and Harriet Martineau. Brougham and Wilderspin were leading exponents of infant schools, while Harriet Martineau achieved fame as a novelist, abolitionist, economist, and social reformer. The following comments of these luminaries typify the judgments of most contemporary liberals.

Lord Brougham and Wilderspin credited Owen with having inspired them to establish infant schools:

In this country, I think it is now seventeen years since, my noble friend Lord Lansdowne and I, with some others, began the first of these seminaries, borrowing the plan, as well as the teachers, from Mr. Owen's manufactory at New Lanark![19]

It may be proper for me to show to whom the public are indebted for the establishment of the first Infant School. I do not know with whom the idea first originated, nor do I think it of much importance to know this; the point is, who first brought it into action? The first Infant School that we heard of in this country was established at Westminster in the year 1819; the master of that institution is J. Buchanan, who came from Mr. Owen's establishment at New Lanark, where an Infant School had been previously formed by that gentleman. As far as I know, Mr. Owen is the first person with whom the idea originated of educating infant children upon an extensive scale . . . . He [Owen] has been pleased to express his approbation of the system there [Spitalfields] pursued, and during these visits has given many useful hints, for which I beg most humbly to thank him; and here I may observe, that I could not have brought the school to its present state had I not received some assistance.[20]

Harriet Martineau emphasized the extraordinary reach of Owen's wide influence:

In spite of his [Owen's] Liberalism, emperors and kings and absolute statesmen went to Lanark, or invited Mr. Owen to their Courts. In spite of his infidelity [to the established church], prelates and their clergy, and all manner of Dissenting Leaders, inspected his schools. In spite of the horror of old bigots and new economists, territories were offered to him [Owen] in various parts of the world on which to try his schemes on a large scale.[21]

CHAPTER 12

Critique

J OHN Locke, the great British philosopher of the seventeenth century, formulated significant theories of political democracy and advocated educational programs based on the practical needs of people and their ability to learn from experience. Rousseau, who was indebted to Locke for fundamental ideas, inspired in the eighteenth century revolutionary movements which swept away old institutions and cleared the path to political democracy and educational reforms. Robert Owen knew little of philosophy and rejected violent revolution, preferring to devote himself to the constructive task of promoting a democratic society and school based on ideals: freedom, self-discipline, and cooperation. His theories were based on personal observation, and rested on a foundation of unflappable optimism. The ease with which he expected his proposals to be put into action demonstrated a certain naïveté. Nevertheless, like Locke and Rousseau, he combined proposals for social reform with those for educational change, insisting that both society and education must be transformed so as to conform to social realities and high moral principles.

I   *Opposition to Owen's Premises*

Owen was criticized by contemporaries more severely for his visionary moral aims and his steadfast determination to remake the world and all people than for his theories of education. Critics scoffed at his concept of an ideal human nature. The Duke of Saxe-Weimer, after visiting the experiment at New Harmony, observed that Owen "looks forward to nothing less than to remodel the world entirely; to root out all crime; to abolish all punishment; to create similar views and similar wants, and in this manner to avoid all dissension and warfare."[1] To such critics the whole Owenite scheme

146

seemed totally impractical and unrealistically far-reaching. Although Owen's views on education were on occasion ridiculed by critics, most of them confined their objections to specific procedures, as, for example, military drill and dancing, which they thought to be frivolous, to the neglect of Bible study, which they attributed to an immoral or unchristian attitude, or to the course of study for girls, which they considered either unladylike or unnecessary. Rarely, however, were Owen's underlying premises and basic methods of education attacked.

Many who criticized Owen did so in defense of the status quo, attempting to rationalize their role within the existing social system, often as fervently devoted to its preservation as Owen was to its revision or elimination. Those ranking at the top of the social hierarchy were understandably zealous to protect their interests. Clergymen attacked Owen for failing to accept traditional rituals and procedures—from which they derived their sustenance—and for commenting adversely on their methods of educating youth. Industrialists were impelled to respond vehemently to Owen's suggestion that their motivation was too often greed, their ideal materialism, and their method exploitation. He had tried to convince them that, just as machines perform better if well cared for, the same should be true of human beings employed in their establishments. He pointed to the results of the experiment at New Lanark which showed that profits increase when living conditions of workers improve, but few manufacturers were convinced. Since most of them felt that "pampering" the employees might reduce profits, they hastened to refute Owen's theories and reject his proposals.

From the very beginning of his philanthropic efforts, Owen met with opposition from a variety of sources, including even his personal friends. Concerning the days when his experiments were still in the planning stage, he wrote: "When to my friends and nearest companions I mentioned that my intentions were to commence a new system of management [at New Lanark] on principles of justice and kindness, and gradually to abolish punishment in governing the population,—they, one and all, smiled at what they called my simplicity, in imagining I could succeed in such a hopeless impossiblity."[2]

But Owen persevered in the firm belief that once the success of his policy had been witnessed, it would win countless converts to his way of thinking. Attacks on his communities, on his moral beliefs, and on his system of education proved to be a source of frustration for him more on account of the lack of empathy they signified than on account of any personal loss of esteem. Because Owen was aware of the controversy he created, in his autobiography he set up a hypothetical question and answer section between an "inquisitor" and himself. Here he presented the prevailing views of his reputation and his own appraisal of his contribution to society.

Inquisitor—You [Owen] are an enigma to everyone, and no one knows what to make of you, and therefore some say you are a visionary, some that you are impractical, some that you are insane, some that you are mad, and the Jesuits say that you are too bad a man to be allowed to appear among the worst characters in the late Madame Tussaud's gallery of the worst outcasts of society.
My [Owen's] experience leads me to know that by such kind of madmen, who had sufficient moral courage to disregard public opinion and all the prejudices of their age, the greatest discoveries have been made, and the greatest benefits have been secured for humanity.[3]

Owen declared that society, "based as it is on a glaring universal falsehood", was inevitably "incompetent to train, educate, and place a human being to become a good and great man."[4] This negative assessment of the effects of an errant society on succeeding generations presented a seemingly insurmountable problem to Owen. If he were raised in that inadequate system, how could his character remain untainted and, furthermore, how could his doctrines be other than erroneous? Owen chose to sidestep that issue: "You must think of me [Owen] as not belonging to the present system of society, but as one looking with the greatest delight to its entire annihilation, so that ultimately not one stone of it shall be left upon another."[5]

Never did Owen modify his theories owing to adverse criticism but, on the contrary, grew more adamant in advocacy of them through the years, embellishing and extending them to encompass not merely a community, nor a single nation, but the entire world. To the end he expected that his plans would be recognized as valid proposals for immediate adoption and implementation by world leaders.

He knew, however, that very few people shared his views on human nature and therefore felt himself to be on the defensive when, in responding to criticism, he discussed the possibility that he might be in error in such conclusions. A vast majority could be wrong, a tiny minority could be right, he declared: "The chances then, you will say, are greatly against me. True: but the chances have been equally against every individual who has been enabled to make any discovery whatever."[6] He thought of himself as a prophet whose vision had not yet been recognized as truth. His critics could not persuade him nor could he convince them, so that both sides generally became emotionally involved in debate from which neither derived benefit.

Owen learned to anticipate a certain amount of hostility to his theories and to accept it philosophically. "It is a law of nature, that that which is new and different to established institutions and previous habits, shall be, at first, opposed, and opposed with virulence and violence in proportion to its newness, and to the prejudices or ignorance of the parties to whom the discovery is stated, until they can be taught to comprehend it."[7]

He was willing to devote his lifetime to wearing down his opponents and convincing them of their errors and the validity of his arguments. *The Times* of London reprimanded him for his repetitiveness, yet admitted that his style was forceful.

Mr. Owen introduced the topic of the day by a speech, in which he rather applied himself to resume and reassert his own former propositions, than attempted to explain them by any novelty of illustration, or to enforce them by any reasonings yet untried . . . . The spirit which animates Mr. Owen is such as to gain admirers among those who are not converts to his theory, and to render nearly powerless against him those whose bitterness it cannot disarm.[8]

The Times criticized Owen further for not detailing his plans, but expecting his enthusiasm to convince people of the merit of his plans. *The Times* considered Owen's schemes suspect primarily because they dealt with "the infinite perfectibility of man, during a finite life."[9] On one occasion he suggested, however, in rebuttal, that either he or the world was insane, and surely it was not he, for insanity entails inconsistency and he had been developing and carrying out the same plans steadily and successfully for many years. Since he had always been stable and unwavering in his convictions, he could not be adjudged insane, whereas the world must be so adjudged in view of its myriad of inconsistencies.

II   Reactions to Owen's Personality

Robert Dale Owen conceded that his father never acquired much knowledge about the works of traditional authorities in the areas of his interest and contended that this was why Robert Owen often claimed to have originated ideas that had already been propounded by eminent thinkers and could be found in well-known sources. Owen had no conscious intention of appropriating the ideas of others without acknowledging indebtedness to them, but, when critics accused him of this offense, he could only repeat his arguments confidently and dogmatically, ignoring any possibility that insuperable obstacles in the world of reality might render his proposals impractical and futile. His attitude of confident self-assertion and invincibility made him vulnerable to attacks of critics directed at his personality rather than at his theories.

Thus Francis Place, the influential social reformer, active in the Royal Lancasterian Society, who agreed with Owen on many points and helped him to organize the *Essays on the Formation of Character,* commented:

I found him [Owen] a man of kind manners and good intentions, of an imperturbable temper, and an enthusiastic desire to promote the happiness of mankind . . . . Mr. Owen then was, and is still, persuaded that he was the first who had ever observed that man was the creature of circumstances. On this supposed discovery he founded his system. Never having read a metaphysical book, nor held a metaphysical conversation, nor having even heard of the disputes respecting freewill and necessity, he had no clear conception of his subject, and his views were obscure. Yet he has all along been preaching and publishing and projecting and predicting in the fullest conviction that he could command circumstances or create them, and place men above their control when necessary. He never was able to explain these absurd notions, and therefore always required assent to them, telling those who were not willing to take his words on trust that it was their ignorance which prevented them from at once assenting to these self-evident propositions.[10]

Owen's confident assertion that within six months the conditions of society in Great Britain would be altered to conform with his suggestions and experiments seemed highly comical to Place, who reacted with tongue-in-cheek tolerance and concealed amusement, just as many other critics did. Nevertheless, although Place's writings and other criticisms sometimes highlighted Owen's personality quirks and questioned his judgment, there was never any doubt that Owen was motivated only by an earnest desire to benefit humanity.

In fact, Owen had formed the habit of reiterating each assertion over and over in essays and addresses, devoting most of his time to mere repetition as if that proved him to be right. He himself realized that he had been accused of being a man possessed by a fixed idea. The noted English essayist William Hazlitt (1778 - 1830) said of him:

There are people who have but one idea: at least, if they have more, they keep it a secret, for they never talk but of one subject.[11]

Mr. Owen is a man remarkable for one idea. It is that of himself and the Lanark cottonmills. He carries this idea backwards and forwards with him from Glasgow to London, without allowing any thing for attrition, and expects to find it in the same state of purity and perfection in the latter place as at the former. He acquires a wonderful velocity and impenetrability in his undaunted transit. Resistance to him is vain, while the whirling motion of the mail-coach remains in his head:[12]

Although Hazlitt deprecated Owen's inflexible attitude, it is apparent from his criticism that he expected his readers to be familiar with Owen and aware of his theories.

The British social reformer George Jacob Holyoake (1817 - 1906), who knew Owen and agreed with his principles, described him in a much more favorable light. Holyoake declared that Owen's manners and charm impressed all who met him, that Owen had a "natural nobility" and air of authority, a vivacity and sense of humor that made him an excellent speaker whose speeches were more interesting than his writings. Holyoake wrote: "Just as Thomas Paine was the founder of political ideas among the people of England, Robert Owen was also the founder of social ideas among them."[14] Owen's greatest contribution, said Holyoake, was putting those social ideas into practice at New Lanark, and he credited Owen with being the first to suggest a "science of society"[15] or social science. According to Holyoake, Owen easily converted people to his way of thinking because of the soundness of his ideas and because he could "speak on the platform impressively and with a dignity of force which commanded the admiration of cultivated adversaries."[16] But even Holyoake admitted the complaint of other critics that later in life Owen had become "a somewhat tiresome reformer. His letters were essays and his speeches were volumes. When he called a meeting together, those who attended never knew when they would separate."[17] On the other hand, despite tiresome repetitiveness, Owen retained the respect of most people, including Holyoake, because he was plainly a "man of veracity and reflection"[18] who had to be much admired for his sincerity and integrity.

III   Opposition to Owen's Religious Views

Nearly all clergymen of his time opposed Robert Owen's candid opinions concerning the shortcomings of organized religion. The reactions of the Scottish minister John Brown were typical of the profession. Brown disapproved of Owen's "radical" views, but without being able adequately to refute them. He rejected Owen's argument that men ought never to be held accountable for their deeds: "If men are *nothing* but what circumstances over which they have no control have made them, then virtue and crime are empty names."[19] Here Brown was hitting at one of Owen's basic premises, namely, that, since people are not directly responsible for their actions, virtue and crime cannot be equitably dealt with, and punishment and reward have no value. Consequently, Owen forbade the use of punishments and rewards in his schools. But clergymen were unable to reconcile religious doctrines with the conclusion that punishments and rewards are useless, for their religion taught them human behavior in this life would be evaluated and either punished or rewarded in the next world.

Even staunch religionists critical of Owen's premises had to admit, however, that at New Lanark "to a certain amount, a change to the better has taken place."[20] Brown's rationalizations, on the other hand, typified the weak arguments of most clergymen in the face of Owen's obvious good intentions and benevolence:

Free as our strictures have been, we cannot conclude without expressing our sincere respect for Mr. Owen, and our equally sincere regret that he should have entangled himself so deeply in the mazes of error. We find it impossible to survey that ardent wish for human happiness, so like Christian benevolence, which breathes in all that he writes and speaks, and which his munificent donations and active exertions sufficiently prove to be sincere, especially when we connect this with his strict integrity and spotless honour in private life, without loving him, and saying "surely this man cannot be far from the kingdom of God." As the best way of proving the truth of our profession, though at the hazard of exciting the smile of derision on the countenance of the object of our good wishes, should he chance to glance at these pages, we most ardently beseech the Father of light, and the Author of knowledge (and, persuaded that "prayers of righteous men avail much," we intreat all our pious readers to join us in the supplication) that he would open his understanding to understand the Scriptures, and, shining into his heart, give him the light of the knowledge of the glory of God as it is in the face of Christ Jesus.[21]

Brown's criticism is more like a sermon than a rebuttal, omitting any rational analysis of Owen's ideas. Brown was interested in reconverting Owen to Christianity rather than in refuting his principles. In the absence of convincing intellectual or practical arguments, the clergy usually had recourse to mystical and emotional appeals as a means of counteracting Owen's views on religion and religious education, and in the increasingly skeptical, materialistic climate of the new industrial age, such appeals were more often than not unsuccessful. Church leaders persisted in their opposition to Owen, however, for acceptance of his characterization of religions as "geographic insanities" would have meant the loss of self-esteem and an acknowledgement of the ineffectualness of their lives.

Owen's followers repeatedly offered their rebuttal to the clerical attacks. In 1832 *The Crisis*[22]—a journal edited by Robert Owen and Robert Dale Owen—defended Owen's contention that human character is formed for man by the environment, not by the individual, and denied that such a view reduces men to machines and encourages disregard for the propriety of their conduct. The journal pointed out that, although man's character is formed for him, it is continually being modified by his fellow men:

To believe that the character is formed for the individual, does not by any means prevent us from estimating the quality of his actions; it only gives us a clue to their origin, and directs us to the means by which to render them such as we desire they should be. Again, even though impressed with the idea that a child has had no share in creating his thoughts and feelings, we should be perfectly justified in expressing to him our opinion of his actions, that we might thereby give him a motive either to repeat or to alter them according as they were good or bad. There is no inconsistency with our first principle in this mode of acting, because the feeling of approval or disapproval, is equally excited within us, whether the child or individual has, or has *not* originated his own thoughts and feelings.[23]

In other words, even though a person's character is formed for him, he still suffers the consequences of his behavior and therefore learns to modify that behavior so that it will become acceptable to fellow human beings. In the end, each person benefits from conduct that makes his companions happy, for they will reciprocate by striving to make him happy. The individual must be taught "while he is yet a child, to acquire the *habit* . . . of calculating consequences, and preferring future permanent benefit to a temporary gratification."[24]

IV   *Conclusion*

Robert Owen was a man of his time but also ahead of his time, a man of vision who used his resources and influence to advance causes such as child labor laws, cooperative communities, the socialist movement, a just and democratic society, public health and welfare, and innovative, enlightened national systems of free, universal education for all classes, children, and adults. A great many of his ideas and proposals have become commonplace achievements in the modern world. It is no surprise when writings of scholars in our own times echo many of Owen's "radical" theories, as in statements that a major purpose of education should be "a commitment and a program to develop character,"[25] and that the school, filling gaps created in the home, should strive to preserve in youth the moral values regarded as fundamental by Robert Owen: "honesty and truthfulness . . . trustworthiness . . . work well done . . . kindness and compassion . . . the courage to admit mistakes . . . racial tolerance . . . respect for law . . . nonviolence . . . respect for democratic rights."[26]

Assessing Owen's contributions to society, Holyoake called him "a standard-bearer of advanced opinions,"[27] and explained why so many people and institutions should be grateful for them:

Children owe him [Owen] thanks, for he founded infant schools . . . workmen owe him thanks, for he set the example of shorter hours of labour; Prussia owes him thanks, for he was the author of their national system of education; . . . Politicians who believe in progress without war, owe him thanks, for he insisted upon international arbitration before Peace Societies were ventured upon; Co-operators owe him thanks, for he it was who taught them how to economise the expenditure of their earnings; Teachers owe him thanks, for he first developed the plan of normal schools; the People owe him thanks, for he first suggested those schemes of social recreation, and those attentions to their physical condition, which are now the recognised duty of the highest classes to promote . . . . He took a wise and wide interest in the welfare of the people, beyond any other leader of opinion. He had no contemporary, and he leaves no successor.[28]

Holyoake praised Owen's educational innovations, stating: "No middle-class gentleman in those days ever thought of giving his family such opulent education as Owen gave his workpeople."[29] Owen's problem, said Holyoake, was that he dreamed of "world making,"[30] thereby setting himself an impossible task, constantly devoting himself to the service of the people and striving to make the world better for all by means of improved living conditions, a better environment, more knowledge and skill, more enjoyable leisure and recreation, more happiness.

Over a century has passed since Harriet Martineau, Owen's contemporary, attempted to strike a balance between positive and negative evaluations of Owen's work: "As long as the name of Robert Owen continues to be heard of there will be some to laugh at it, but there will be more to love and cherish it. The probability seems to be that time will make his prodigious errors more palpable and unquestionable; but that it will at least in equal proportion exalt his name and fame, on account of some great intuitive truths which are at present about equally involved with his wildest mistakes and his noblest virtues."[31] But even the liberal-minded Harriet Martineau probably underestimated Robert Owen whose mistakes have, by and large, been forgotten while his truths, so influential during the past century, are still being reexamined and found to be in good standing today.

Robert Dale Owen's
Sample Lessons

Robert Dale Owen demonstrated in the following appendix his father's system of education. He presented a series of sample lessons, revolving around what today might be called a "core curriculum," that is, educational matter being presented in various subjects connected by a single theme. The theme common to all these lessons is the earth. Beginning with a description of the physical properties of the earth, Robert Dale Owen illustrates how such a topic could be integrated into lessons in all subjects and made relevant to the children's experience. Even seemingly unconnected fields such as art, music, and mathematics are used to further the children's knowledge and comprehension of the subject matter.

Owen's lessons proceeded from the known to the unknown, from the concrete to the abstract. The teacher would begin by telling the children briefly what they would learn later to arouse their interest and to present them with an informal outline to which they could refer as the lesson unraveled. He would bring in simple visual aids to illustrate his points. He would draw carefully thought out analogies to show clearly the nature of the object studied. He would emphasize relationships between familiar items and the new material, in this case an orange and the earth. Wherever possible, the teacher would relate the material to the children's daily lives, as in the explanation of the study of zoology and architecture. Although this appendix does not allow space for pupils' questions, Owen believed that was a fundamental part of any lesson, and urged his teachers to be flexible enough to expand or contract the time allotted for each lesson in accordance with the children's interest.

The teacher could easily adapt these lessons to fit the needs of various age groups.

Such well-planned lessons call into question Owen's claim that spontaneity prevailed in his classrooms. Note that these sample lessons were modeled after the lessons given at New Lanark in Robert Owen's Institute for the Formation of Character.

APPENDIX[1]

The following brief "Introduction to the Arts and Sciences," is presented to the public merely to explain what sort of outline it is here recommended to give to children, before entering into further details. It was drawn up for the New Lanark Schools, and has been communicated to the older classes. The teachers are directed to illustrate each idea by any anecdote or interesting particular, which may occur to them, or by drawings or models; and to encourage the children, after hearing a short portion of it, to repeat and explain that portion in familiar language. This they are generally able to do with considerable facility.

A manuscript of this "Introduction" has been transcribed by some of the elder scholars, in order at once to impress it on their minds, and to improve their style of hand-writing.

THE EARTH

On which we live, is a very large ball. It is nearly round, in the shape of a globe. The hills and mountains on its surface, even the highest and largest of them, which are six or seven times higher than any mountain in Great Britain, do not prevent the earth's being round, any more than the roughness on the skin of an orange prevents the orange being round; for they are not so large compared to the whole earth, as the small raised parts, which make the orange skin rough compared to the orange. And, therefore, if we were going to represent the earth by a globe as large as an orange, we should not make the mountains so large as these small inequalities on the skin of the orange.

The earth does not seem to us round, but flat, because we can only see a very, very small part of the outside of the earth at once;

and a small part of the outside of a large ball is so very like a flat surface, that we cannot easily distinguish it from one. But we know that the earth *is* round, because people, by travelling for two or three years, in the same direction, came at last to the place they set out from. These people travelled round the world.

We do not know whether the earth is solid or not; because we have never seen the inside, except a very short way under the surface.

It is always turning round with us. Yet we do not feel it moving, because every thing we see moves along with us. In the same way, that if a ship sails on a smooth sea, and we are in one of the rooms in the inside of the ship, we cannot tell whether the ship is moving or not; for it does not seem to us to move at all.

The earth is warmed by a much larger globe than itself, called the sun. The sun is a very great way from the earth. If it were too near, everything would be burnt up. If the sun did not give us heat, nothing could grow or live.

A candle, or any light, can only shine on one half of a globe at a time; the other half is dark. In the same way, the sun can only shine on one half of the earth at once, while the other half, on which it cannot shine, must be dark. This is the reason why it is sometimes day, and sometimes night. The part of the earth we are on, is turned to the sun in the daytime, and turned away from it at night.

You will be told afterwards, why the days are sometimes longer, and sometimes shorter; and why it is hot in summer, and cold in winter.

If you were going to draw a picture of a ball, you could only draw one half of it at once. Then you would require to turn it round, and draw the other half. That is the reason why the whole earth is drawn on two hemispheres. As you cannot draw it round on paper, it seems flat, but each hemisphere should in fact be a half ball. Every other map, although all maps are drawn flat, represents a part of the outside of the large ball we live on, so that, to be quite correct, it should be raised from the paper.

The world, or any part of the world, can be drawn on a very large map, or on a very small one, in the same way that you can draw the same house on a large piece of paper, and make it large, or on a small piece, and make it small. This is called drawing on a *large scale*, or on a *small scale*.

Part of the outside of the earth is covered with water. The part that is not covered with water is called land, and is not quite half as large as the other.

The whole of the outside of the earth is, therefore, either land or water.

The whole of the earth is surrounded by air.

EVERY thing that is in, or on the earth, is called a *substance*. Each of these substances is supposed to consist of very small particles, much too small to be seen.

All these substances remain on, or in the earth, and the different parts of each of them keep together;—because all substances are drawn towards each other, we do not know how or why.

The larger a substance is, the more it draws another to it; because it has more particles than a smaller body, and each of these particles draws a little. This is the reason why the earth draws every substance to itself; or, in other words, why substances *fall* if we let them; and why they *press* with what is called their *weight*, upon any thing that supports them.

When any body falls, it draws the earth a *very* little upwards, in the same way that the earth draws it downwards. But all bodies are so small compared to the earth, and the earth is so large, compared to them, that we do not see the earth fall to them, or move towards them, and they fall to it.

The different substances on the earth would fall towards each other if they were larger than the earth; but we never see them do so, because none of them are nearly so large as the earth; and, therefore, although they *are* drawn to each other, yet the earth draws them towards itself so much more forcibly, that they are held down to the earth, and cannot fall towards each other.

This is the reason that it requires an effort to raise one of our arms or legs, and that it falls again if we let it.

This is the reason, too, why we never fall off the earth when it is turning round; for (because the earth draws us strongly towards itself,) we always remain standing, or sitting, or lying on it. *We call that which is* IN *the earth,* BELOW *us; and we say, that that which surrounds the earth,* (for instance, the clouds,) *is* ABOVE *us. Therefore,* however the earth turns, we always stand or sit with our feet downwards, and our heads upwards; that is, with our feet turned towards the earth, and our heads away from it.

If a larger substance than the earth were to come near the earth, it would draw the earth to it; that is, the earth, and everything that is upon the earth, would fall to it; but although there *are* many larger substances than the earth, which you will be told about afterwards, they are not near enough to draw the earth to them.

For, the *nearer* substances are to each other, the more strongly they are drawn together. This is the reason why the small particles of every thing or substance remain together, and why it requires force to separate, cut, or divide any thing.

This inclination of substances to fall toward each other, is called *attraction;* and when they are drawn together, we say they attract each other.

If substances did not attract each other, any power, that could set them, even in the least degree in motion, (for instance, the wind,) would blow every thing to pieces; and the whole world would be separated into small particles in a very short time.

Whenever the force of the wind on a substance is stronger than the attraction *of the earth* to that substance, then the substance is lifted into the air; and whenever the attraction becomes stronger than the force of the wind, it falls again.

Whenever the force of the wind on the particles of a substance is stronger than the attraction of these particles *to each other*, then that substance is blown to pieces.

Whenever the attraction of the particles of a body or substance *to the earth* is stronger than their attraction *to each other,* then that body falls to pieces; that is, each of the separate particles the body is made of falls to the earth, *as soon as the* SIZE *of the earth makes the attraction greater, than the* CLOSENESS *of these small particles to each other, makes it.* For the force of the attraction always depends on the *closeness* of the bodies, and on their *size.*

Almost all bodies, which we see, are made of two or more substances, and are then called *compound* bodies. The substances these compound bodies are made of, are called *elements,* or *simple bodies.* We very seldom find simple bodies; that is, we very seldom find bodies made of one substance only.

Although there are so *very* many compound bodies, yet there are very few different kinds of simple bodies, but the different ways in which these bodies come together, make the different objects we see; in the same way that, although there are so few letters in the alphabet, you can make so very many words by putting them together.

We can decompose all compound bodies; that is, we can find out the simple bodies they are made of, but we cannot always put the simple bodies together again, so as to form the compounds we decomposed; for instance, we can decompose flesh or bones, and get the simple substances they are made of; but after we have got these, we cannot make flesh and bones of them again.

Every substance belongs to one of the three great divisions called Kingdoms, viz.—

The Animal Kingdom;

The Vegetable Kingdom; and

The Mineral Kingdom.

Now, I will tell you how you can generally find out to which kingdom any thing belongs.

ANIMALS change, live, move of themselves, and (most of them, if not all,) think.

VEGETABLES change, live, (cannot move of themselves, and are not supposed to think.)

MINERALS change, (do not live, therefore cannot die or fade, cannot, any more than vegetables, move of themselves, or think.)°

Therefore, animals, vegetables, and minerals, or all substances—change; animals and vegetables change and live; animals change, live, move of themselves, and think.

I. HOW ANIMALS, VEGETABLES, AND MINERALS, CHANGE.

ALL substances are continually changing, either slowly, or quickly; sometimes increasing; sometimes decreasing; sometimes with little or no change that we can perceive; sometimes by means of an instant and complete change. When animals or vegetables change, so as to increase in size, we say they *grow.*

When an *animal* is born, it is smaller than it will be after it has lived some time. It continues to increase in size, or to grow; sometimes only for some hours; sometimes for many years, till it has

---

°These divisions and definitions are given, not because they were considered the most critically correct that could be adopted, but because they were thought to be simple, and easy of application.

attained its full size. Still, however, the different particles of the
animal continue moving about, and becoming altered; and the
whole body and appearance becomes changed, but slowly. Animals
grow so slowly that we cannot see them growing; but we see after
some time, that they have become larger, and that their appearance
has become altered.

Vegetables begin to grow from a seed, or from a root, when this
seed or root is put into the earth, or sometimes when it is merely put
into water. Some parts of vegetables grow upwards; those are the
parts we see; some downwards into the earth, and these are called
roots. Vegetables grow in general more quickly than animals, but
still they scarcely ever grow so quickly, that we can see them
growing.—Most vegetables grow during the hot months of the year;
and cease to grow, and even lose part of their growth, in winter.
The particles a vegetable is made of, move about in it, and become
gradually altered, as well as those of an animal. Some vegetables
grow much larger than any animals.

Minerals change, as well as animals and vegetables, but in a very
different manner to these, and *very* much slower, often without
seeming to change at all. Some of them, however, become many
thousand times larger than any animal or vegetable. The whole
body of the earth, as far as we know, is composed of minerals, which
have been changing for a very long time.

There are a very great many more mineral substances in the earth
than animal or vegetable substances; for animal and vegetable substances grow merely on the surface of the earth, whereas, the earth
itself is probably made of mineral substances.

II.   HOW ANIMALS AND VEGETABLES LIVE.

You have just been told, that animals, vegetables, and minerals,
are continually changing,—sometimes growing larger, sometimes
becoming less; but you know, that animals and vegetables grow
quite in a different way from minerals. First of all, they grow
quicker; then, animals cannot grow unless they are fed, nor
vegetables unless they are planted. Then again, animals and
vegetables grow larger for a certain time; then they continue nearly
the same size; then they become less and less vigorous, till at last
they always change completely, and become what we call *dead*. The

animal does not move about then, nor take food, as it used to do; the vegetable does not grow in the warm months, and lose its growth in the cold ones, as it used to do. It falls to the ground; and the roots and branches of the dead vegetable, and the body of the dead animal, gradually fall to pieces, and mix with the minerals and vegetables around them, and change along with them.

Now, this way in which animals and vegetables change till they die, is called *living*; and the sudden change they all undergo, when they no longer continue this mode of existence, is called *death*. Minerals do not grow in this way for a time, and then change suddenly; therefore, minerals do not live or die.

Animals cannot live without eating food, which is either an animal, vegetable, or mineral substance, chiefly a vegetable one; nor without drawing in and breathing out the air with which the earth is surrounded. If they are without food or air, for a short time, almost all animals will die. This food, and this air, must be proper for the animal, or he cannot live either. Some animals eat one kind of food, and some another. Each different species of animals requires different kinds of food to keep it alive. Some kinds of air, too, would kill an animal, if he were to breathe them: these are sometimes found a little below the surface of the earth. But the air which surrounds the earth is, almost everywhere, fit for breathing; only it is better in one place than another.

Part of the food an animal eats, mixes with the particles of the body of the animal; and the air the animal breathes takes away some of these particles. These particles are thus continually in motion, so as gradually to change the animal. Most animals have blood, which is red in some, and white in others. It moves about in the body of the animal as long as it lives. If a severe blow or stab prevent these things from going on, the animal is killed.

Some animals do not live for one day; others live for about 200 years. We do not know what is the longest time some animals may live.

Vegetables cannot live, any more than animals, without food, nor without air. Their roots receive nourishment from the ground, or from water, and this nourishment is circulated all over the vegetable. The other parts of the vegetable, particularly the leaves, are acted upon by the air which surrounds it, so that circulation is continually going on throughout the vegetable. Some vegetables require one kind of ground, and some another. Some vegetables live only one summer, and these are called *annuals;* some live longer probably than any animals; some are said to have lived about 1000 years.

If a vegetable be cut in two, that part which remains in the ground generally continues to live, and the other part dies.

Some animals and vegetables can only live in warm countries, and some few only in cold ones.

III.   HOW ANIMALS *MOVE* AND *THINK*.

SOME animals move on land, and some in water. Most land animals move about by means of feet, which they put forwards and backwards as they please. A few land animals move without feet, by drawing their bodies together, and then stretching them out again. Some land animals can move about in the air, without touching the land, by means of wings, with which they continue to strike the air, as long as they wish to move about. Water animals move about in the water, by means of fins, which are grisly substances, which they can move at pleasure, so as to answer the purpose of our feet. Only one kind of water animal that we know, can move about in the air, and it can only do so for a short time.

Most animals have five senses; viz. the senses of seeing, hearing, feeling, smelling, tasting. Every thing that surrounds them makes an impression on the senses, perhaps somewhat in the same way that we can make an impression on any thing, for instance by strik-ing or pressing it. If we strike or press any thing it receives the stroke or pressure; and if any thing comes before our eyes, our eyes receive the image or impression of that thing. If they did not, we could not see what it was like;—and the same with the rest of their senses.

We certainly do not know *how* our senses get these impressions, but we know that they *do* get them; for we see things with our eyes, hear with our ears, feel with our fingers and other parts of our bodies, smell with our noses, and taste with our mouths. If we could not see, hear, smell, taste or feel, we could know nothing of what is about us; so that every thing we know, we know by our senses. We could not think at all if we knew nothing, and we always think ac-cording to what we know, or according to these impressions.

Therefore these impressions give us thought, and after we have thoughts, then we move about or act. So that you see the impressions which we receive by our senses, cause us to move about or act.

Now Vegetables have not these senses. They do not see, hear, feel, smell or taste. Therefore they can neither think, nor move about, nor act.

Now I will tell you what are the different kinds of knowledge, which have been obtained by the senses of different men.

All knowledge belongs either to an *art* or a *science*.

Whatever tells us of the nature and properties of any substance, is a *science*.

Whatever teaches us how to produce any thing, is an *art*.

The principal sciences are—

Astronomy, Geography, Mathematics, Zoology, Botany and Mineralogy—Chemistry.

The arts are—

Agriculture, Manufactures, Architecture, Drawing, (including Sculpture,) Music, and a few others of less importance.

Almost all these arts depend upon sciences, for it is necessary to know what are the nature and qualities of substances, before we can produce them.

I am now going to tell you what these sciences tell us about, and what these arts teach us.

ASTRONOMY.

There are, as I told you, many other very large bodies besides the earth, some of them much larger than the earth. These bodies are the sun, the moon and the stars. Astronomy teaches us all that is yet known about them; and about their sizes and distances from one another. They are so far from this earth, that we do not know much about them.

GEOGRAPHY

Is the knowledge of the countries that are on the surface of the earth. It tells us what these different countries are like, and how

they are divided. It tells us of the manners and customs of the people who live in them, and what animals, vegetables and minerals
are found there.

MATHEMATICS

Teaches us how to number and to measure different bodies, and
how to tell their proportionate sizes to each other.

ZOOLOGY

Is the natural history of animals; or the knowledge of the formation, appearance, habits, and dispositions of animals.

As men and women are animals, it tells us about them; for instance, about their bodies, about the blood, flesh, bones, sinews,
joints, and all the different parts of the body. It explains to us, as far
as can yet be explained, how they live, how they move about, how
they feel and think, and how they should be treated; but in all these
things there is a great deal that has not yet been discovered, and
that we cannot understand.

That part of the natural history of men and women, which tells us
what men and women did before we were born and since that time,
is called *History*. We are not sure that all histories are quite true;
because the people who wrote them might have been mistaken, or
might have written that, which they knew did not happen.
However, when different writers of history, who did not know one
another and had not seen what one another wrote, tell us the same
thing, it is more likely to be true, than when only one writer tells us
so.

It is more difficult to tell whether what we read in history is true
or not, than whether what we read about the earth and its productions is true, because we can see the earth, and what is on it, but we
cannot see what happened before we were born; nor if it be long
since, even see the persons, who were there when any event
happened.

That part of Zoology which tells us about men and women, is the
most important science in the world, because you will grow to be
men and women, and then you will find how very useful it is to
know as much as is yet known about yourselves. Now although
every thing you will hear about yourselves does really belong to

Zoology, yet there is so much of it, and it is so very different from the natural history of other animals, that it is generally found convenient not to include it under Zoology, but to divide it into a number of different sciences, which you will hear of when you are older and better able to understand them.

BOTANY

Is the knowledge of all substances that belong to the vegetable kingdom, therefore of all trees, shrubs, flowers, fruits, and other vegetable productions.

MINERALOGY

Is the knowledge of the substances of which the earth is made.

That part of Mineralogy, which tells us about the interior (or inside) of the earth, and about large mineral masses, is called *Geology*.

We know very little about Geology, because we have never been able to get more than two miles into the earth. Now it is 8000 miles through the earth, so that we must have gone 4000 times farther than two miles to see what was all through the earth.

Now I will tell you what the arts are, that I mentioned to you.

AGRICULTURE

The greater part of the food we eat is produced from the ground. Agriculture is the art of producing this food. It is by far the most useful and necessary employment in the world, because we could scarcely live without it.

MANUFACTURES

Every thing we wear and every thing we use, except food, is produced by manufactures. The greater part of these things is made by machines. One machine often does as much work as a great many men and women. New machines are found out almost every day.

Small manufactures are often called trades; for instance the trade of a shoemaker, tailor, &c.

ARCHITECTURE

Is the art of building the houses in which men and women live. A hut is a very small house which was easily built, and which has only one or two rooms. A palace is a very large house, which contains many rooms, and which costs much trouble in building.

DRAWING

Is the art of representing objects, so that a person who sees the drawing may know what the object is like, although he has never seen the object itself. The more like the drawing seems to the object it is meant to represent, the better it is done. Most drawings are made on paper, canvass or ivory. Drawings of persons are called portraits.

Sculpture is the art of representing objects by cutting wood or stone like them.

MUSIC

Is the art of producing pleasant sounds by means of the voice, or of different instruments. The knowledge of the rules required to compose music is called Thorough Bass.

Most of these sciences might be included under CHEMISTRY; and even many of the arts depend upon it; for Chemistry is, in fact—

The knowledge of the properties of all substances, and of the manner in which all simple substances are combined, and all compound substances decomposed.

Under Chemistry, however, *is generally understood* the knowledge of some of the properties of such of the simple substances as we have already discovered, and of a few of their combinations, as well as the way to make some of these combinations. Even in this contracted signification, Chemistry includes a part of the sciences of Zoology, Botany and Mineralogy. The substances it tells us about at present are chiefly minerals; so that it is the most connected with Mineralogy.

We do not know nearly so much about Chemistry as we may expect to know, when people have paid more attention to it and tried more experiments.

In order to get an easier knowledge of the sciences and arts, we learn to read, write, and to understand languages, the arithmetical signs, and the musical notes and signs. But these are not real knowledge. We only learn them, that we may be able to acquire knowledge by means of them. All real knowledge is not included in any of these, but only in the arts and sciences.

Trade or commerce is the system of arrangements, by which the productions of nature and of the arts are at present distributed.

Any new fact in science is called a *discovery:* any new mode of producing, an *invention.*

No science or art is by any means complete. People are learning something new in all of them almost every day. That is; there are discoveries and inventions made almost every day.

Notes and References

Chapter One

1. Robert Owen, *The Life of Robert Owen by Himself*, preface, pp. xi-xii, hereafter cited as *Owen by Himself*.
2. Robert Owen, *A Discourse on A New System of Society*, pp. 4-5.
3. Robert Dale Owen, *Threading My Way*, p. 42.
4. Ibid., p. 35.
5. *Owen by Himself*, p. 3.
6. Ibid., p. 43.
7. Ibid., p. 7.
8. Frederick Engels, *Socialism: Utopian and Scientific*, p. 67.
9. *Owen by Himself*, p. 63.
10. Ibid., p. 73.
11. Ibid., p. 70.
12. Ibid., p. 69.
13. Ibid., p. 75.

Chapter Two

1. E.P. Thompson, *The Making of the English Working Class*.
2. Rowland Hill Harvey, *Robert Owen Social Idealist*, p. 12.
3. *The Times* (London), June 14, 1824.
4. Robert Owen, *A New View of Society & Other Writings*, p. 122, hereafter cited as *New View of Society*.
5. Ibid., p. 123.
6. Ibid., p. 121.
7. Ibid., p. 124.
8. Ibid., p. 123.
9. Ibid., p. 125.
10. *Owen by Himself*, p. 171.
11. Ibid., p. 172.
12. *New View of Society* p. 156.
13. Ibid., p. 258.
14. Ibid., p. 169.
15. Ibid., p. 164.
16. Ibid., p. 167.
17. *The Times* (London), Aug. 9, 1817.

18. *The Times* (London), July 30, 1817.

19. *New View of Society*, p. 165.

20. Ibid., p. 167.

21. Ibid., p. 164.

22. William Lovett, *The Life and Struggles of William Lovett, in his Pursuit of Bread, Knowledge, and Freedom;* . . ., pp. 43-44.

23. *New View of Society*, p. 180.

24. Ibid., p. 167.

25. Ibid., p. 274.

26. *Owen by Himself*, p. 311.

27. George Jacob Holyoake, *Sixty Years of An Agitator's Life*, p. 122.

28. Ibid., pp. 122-123.

29. Frederick Engels, *Socialism: Utopian and Scientific*, pp. 73-74.

Chapter Three

1. *Robert Owen's Journal*, III, 57 (Nov. 29, 1851), p. 23.

2. *New View of Society*, p. 279.

3. Ibid., pp. 282-283.

4. Ibid., p. 282.

5. *Owen by Himself*, p. 81.

6. *New View of Society*, p. 16. Written in 1813.

7. *Owen by Himself*, p. 181.

8. Harold Silver, ed., *Robert Owen on Education*, p. 203.

9. *New View of Society*, p. 22.

10. *Owen by Himself*, p. 319.

11. *New View of Society*, p. 16.

12. Owen, *Book of the New Moral World*, Third Part, p. 1.

13. Ibid., p. 5.

14. Owen in *The Times* (London), Aug. 9, 1817.

15. *Idem.*

16. *Idem.*

17. *New View of Society*, p. 17.

18. Ibid., p. 51.

19. Ibid., p. 72.

20. The original wording of the title page, as printed in 1813, read *A New View of Society; or, Essays on the Principle of the Formation of the Human Character, and the Application of the Principle to Practice.*

21. *New View of Society*, pp. 54-55.

22. Ibid., p. 56. It is not surprising that in 1813 Owen wrote in the style of many contemporaneous British and American theorists, and thought in terms of happiness much in the style of the Declaration of Independence which preceded his book by less than forty years.

23. Robert Owen, *The Revolution in the Mind and Practice of The Human Race; or . . . ,* preface, p. vii, hereafter cited as *Revolution in the Mind.*

24. *Idem.*

25. Owen in *The Times* (London), Aug. 9, 1817.

Chapter Four

1. *Revolution in the Mind,* p. 5.

2. James Denholm, *The History of the City of Glasgow & Suburbs,* p. 266.

3. Robert Dale Owen, *Threading My Way,* p. 18.

4. Denholm, *History of Glasgow,* p. 266.

5. *Owen by Himself,* p. 80.

6. Ibid., p. 189.

7. *Idem.*

8. *New View of Society,* p. 53.

9. *Owen by Himself,* p. 15.

10. Ibid., p. 87.

11. *New View of Society,* p. 172.

12. Owen, as quoted in George Jacob Holyoake, *The History of Co-operation in England: Its Literature and Its Advocates,* I, pp. 56-57.

13. Robert Dale Owen, "An Outline of the System of Education at New Lanark," in *Robert Owen at New Lanark: Two Booklets and One Pamphlet 1824 - 1838,* pp. 5-6, hereafter cited as "An Outline of the system . . . at New Lanark."

Chapter Five

1. *New View of Society,* p. 16.

2. Ibid., p. 280.

3. *The Crisis,* I, No. 1 (April 14, 1832), p. 3.

4. *New View of Society,* p. 283.

5. Jane Dale Owen, "Jane Dale Owen: The Principles of Natural Education," in *Utopianism and Education: Robert Owen and the Owenites,* John F. C. Harrison, ed., p. 176.

6. *Owen by Himself,* p. 319.

7. *New View of Society,* p. 20.

8. *Revolution in the Mind,* p. 18.

9. *Idem.*

10. *Owen by Himself,* p. 116.

11. *New View of Society,* p. 100.

12. *Idem.*

13. Ibid., p. 113.

14. Adapted from *British Sessional Papers*, 1816, IV, p. 242. Owen submitted these statistics to Parliament when he was testifying on the state of education in England.

15. Robert Dale Owen, "An Outline of the System of Education at New Lanark," p. 5.

16. *Owen by Himself*, p. 115.

17. Ibid., pp. 240-241.

18. *Book of the New Moral World*, Third Part, pp. 12-13.

19. *Owen by Himself*, p. 241.

20. "Jane Dale Owen: The Principles of Natural Education," in op. cit., pp. 180-181.

21. *New View of Society*, p. 280.

22. Ibid., p. 279.

23. *Owen by Himself*, p. 13.

24. *New View of Society*, p. 41.

25. Ibid., pp. 41-42.

26. *Owen by Himself*, p. 193.

27. *Robert Owen's Journal*, III, No. 67 (Feb. 7, 1852), pp. 119-120.

28. *New View of Society*, p. 49.

29. Ibid., p. 280.

Chapter Six

1. Robert Owen, *Book of the New Moral World*, (1836 edition), p. 25.

2. *New View of Society*, p. 82.

3. "An Outline of the System of Education at New Lanark," pp. 9-10.

4. Ibid., p. 132.

5. Ibid., p. 133.

6. *Robert Owen's Journal*, III, No. 67 (Feb. 7, 1852), p. 119.

7. "An Outline of the System of Education at New Lanark," p. 16.

8. Owen, *Book of the New Moral World*, (1836 edition) p. 26.

9. *Owen by Himself*, p. 192.

10. Ibid., p. 191.

11. *Revolution in the Mind*, p. 16.

12. *British Sessional Papers*, 1816, IV, p. 241.

13. *Owen by Himself*, pp. 192 - 193.

14. *Revolution in the Mind*, p. 17.

15. *Idem*.

16. As quoted in Robert R. Rusk, *A History of Infant Education*, pp. 140 - 141.

17. *The Westminster and Foreign Quarterly Review*, 1847, p. 484.

18. *Revolution in the Mind*, p. 17.

19. *Owen by Himself*, p. 197.

20. *Idem*.

21. *Idem*.

Chapter Seven

1. *The Crisis*, I, No. 43 (Dec. 29, 1832), p. 172.

2. *Owen by Himself*, p. 186.

3. *Idem*.

4. Appendix 1, pp. 156 - 169, demonstrates Owen's program of an integrated curriculum.

5. *View of Society*, p. 47.

6. Robert Owen, *A Development of the Principles and Plans on which to establish Self-Supporting Home Colonies; . . ., p. 70*, hereafter cited as *Development of Principles and Plans. . . .*

7. *Owen by Himself*, p. 240.

8. *New View of Society*, p. 48.

9. *Owen by Himself*, p. 278.

10. *New View of Society*, p. 48.

11. "An Outline of the System of Education at New Lanark," p. 71.

12. Robert Dale Owen, *Threading My Way*, p. 166.

13. Owen, *Book of the New Moral World*, Third Part, p. 49.

14. Robert Dale Owen, *Threading My Way*, p. 53.

15. Harold Silver, ed., *Robert Owen on Education*, pp. 192 - 193.

16. *New View of Society*, p. 244.

Chapter Eight

1. *British Sessional Papers*, 1816, IV, p. 238.

2. *Owen by Himself*, p. 147.

3. P. H. J. H. Gosden, *How They Were Taught: An Anthology of Contemporary Accounts of Learning and Teaching in England 1800 - 1950*, p. 7.

4. *Owen by Himself*, p. 59.

5. Ibid., p. 244.

6. Ibid., p. 245.

7. *Idem*.

8. *Owen by Himself*, p. 247.

9. John Dewey, *Democracy and Education*, p. 83.

10. *New View of Society*, p. 74.

11. Ibid., p. 75.

12. *Robert Owen's Journal*, III, No. 53 (Nov. 1, 1851), p. 7.

13. *Owen by Himself*, p. 144.

14. *Idem*.

Chapter Nine

1. *Owen by Himself,* p. 138.
2. *Development of Principles and Plans . . .,* p. 74.
3. *Idem.*
4. Charles Dickens, *The Life & Adventures of Nicholas Nickleby,* preface, p. xv.
5. Ibid., p. 87.
6. Ibid., p. 90.
7. *Development of Principles and Plans . . .,* appendix, p. 24.
8. Robert Owen, *A Discourse on a New System of Society; as delivered in the Hall of Representatives of the United States, . . .* p. 18, hereafter cited as *Discourse on a New System of Society.*
9. *New View of Society,* p. 129.
10. *Idem.*
11. *Development of Principles and Plans . . .,* appendix, p. 24.
12. *Idem.*

Chapter Ten

1. Karl J. R. Arndt, *George Rapp's Harmony Society 1785 - 1847,* p. 292.
2. Robert Owen quoted in George Flower, *History of the English Settlement in Edwards County Illinois, Founded in 1817 and 1818, by Morris Birkbeck and George Flower,* pp. 372 - 373.
3. Ibid., pp. 279 - 280.
4. Owen, "A Discourse on a New System of Society; as delivered in the Hall of Representatives of the United States, . . .," in *Robert Owen in the United States,* Oakley C. Johnson, ed., p. 29.
5. Ibid., p. 22.
6. Ibid., p. 31.
7. William Owen as quoted in Harlow Lindley, ed., *Indiana as Seen By Early Travelers: A Collection of Reprints from Books of Travel, Letters, and Diaries Prior to 1830,* p. 416.
8. *Idem.*
9. *Discourse on a New System of Society,* p. 3.
10. William Hebert in *The Co-operative Magazine and Monthly Herald,* I, No. 1 (Jan., 1826), pp. 13-14.
11. William Hebert, as quoted in Harlow Lindley, ed., *Indiana as Seen By Early Travelers,* p. 338.
12. Donald Macdonald, *The Diaries of Donald Macdonald,* Caroline Dale Snedeker, ed., p. 245.
13. George B. Lockwood, *The New Harmony Movement,* p. 87.

14. William Pelham's phrase in Harlow Lindley, ed., *Indiana as Seen By Early Travelers*, p. 385.

15. Ibid., p. 409.

16. Ibid., p. 370.

17. *The Western Luminary*, Vol. II, No. 33 (Feb. 22, 1826), p. 527.

18. "Discourse on A New System of Society, . . .", in *Robert Owen in the United States*, Oakley C. Johnson, ed., pp. 61-62.

19. Duke of Saxe-Weimar in Harlow Lindley, ed., *Indiana as Seen by Early Travelers*, p. 435.

20. Flower, *History of the English Settlement in Edwards County Illinois*, p. 283.

21. Thomas and Sarah Pears, *New Harmony: An Adventure in Happiness—The Papers of Thomas and Sarah Pears*, Thomas Clinton Pears, Jr., ed., p. 73.

22. Ibid., p. 74.

23. *Idem.*

24. William Maclure in Arthur Bestor, Jr., *Education and Reform at New Harmony: Correspondance of William Maclure and Marie Duclos Fretageot 1820 - 1833*, Sept. 10, 1824, p. 309.

25. Ibid., Aug. 30, 1826, p. 365.

26. Ibid., Feb. 8, 1827, p. 385.

27. Ibid., Jan. 3, 1827, p. 382.

28. Owen, in *New Harmony Gazette*, Vol. III, No. 26 (Apr. 23, 1828), p. 204.

29. Flower, *History of the English Settlement in Edwards County Illinois*, p. 284.

30. Arthur H. Estabrook, "The Family History of Robert Owen," *Indiana Magazine of History*, Vol. XIX, No. 1 (March 1923), p. 69.

31. Ibid., p. 100.

32. Ibid., p. 69.

33. Robert Dale Owen, "An Outline of the System of Education at New Lanark," p. 3.

34. Mrs. David Dale Owen, in *The Diaries of Donald Macdonald 1824 - 1826*, Caroline Dale Snedeker, ed., p. 151.

Chapter Eleven

1. *New View of Society*, pp. 100 - 101.

2. Owenite communities in America in the 1820s included the Forestville Community in Coxsackie, New York (1826 - 1827), the Valley Forge Community in Pennsylvania (1826), the Wanborough Cooperative Association (1825), the Blue Spring Community in Indiana (1826 - 1827), and the Maxwell Community in Ontario, Canada (1827).

3. James M'Knight, *A Discourse Exposing Robert Owen's System, as Practised by the Franklin Community at Haverstraw*, p. 12.

4. *The Crisis*, I, No. 1 (April 14, 1832), p. 1.

5. *The Crisis*, II, No. 1 (Jan. 12, 1833), p. 6.

6. *Book of the New Moral World*, First Part, p. xviii.

7. *The Crisis*, II, No. 1 (Jan. 12, 1833), p. 6.

8. Owen in *The Crisis*, I, No. 30 (Sept. 29, 1832), p. 119.

9. *The Crisis*, II, No. 1 (Jan. 12, 1833), p. 7.

10. Robert Dale Owen, *Threading My Way*, p. 114.

11. *Owen by Himself*, appendix, p. 203.

12. "Discourse on A New System of Society; . . .," in *Robert Owen in the United States*, Oakley C. Johnson, ed., p. 25.

13. *Owen by Himself*, p. 238.

14. William Maclure to Marie Fretageot, London, August 25, 1824, in Arthur Bestor, Jr., *Education and Reform at New Harmony;* p. 307.

15. *Owen by Himself*, p. 277.

16. *The Times* (London), Sept. 10, 1817.

17. Mrs. Frances Trollope, *Domestic Manners of the Americans*, pp. 207 - 208.

18. Flower, *History of the English Settlement in Edwards County Illinois*, p. 282.

19. Lord Brougham, May 1835, as quoted in *Owen by Himself*, appendix, p. 336.

20. Samuel Wilderspin, 1825, as quoted in *Owen by Himself*, appendix, p. 336.

21. Harriet Martineau, *Biographical Sketches*, p. 309.

Chapter Twelve

1. Duke of Saxe-Weimer, as quoted in Harlow Lindley, ed., *Indiana as Seen By Early Travelers*, p. 428.

2. *Owen by Himself*, p. 83.

3. *Owen by Himself* (1967 ed.), pp. xxx-xxxi.

4. Ibid., p. xxi.

5. Ibid., p. xxii.

6. Owen, "An Address to the Inhabitants of New Lanark," in *New View of Society*, p. 114.

7. *Book of the New Moral World*, Seventh Part, p. 42.

8. *The Times* (London), Aug. 15, 1817.

9. Ibid., Sept. 10, 1817.

10. Francis Place, as quoted in Graham Wallas, *The Life of Francis Place 1771 - 1854*, p. 63.

11. William Hazlitt, *Table Talk: Opinions on Books, Men, and Things,* part I, p. 36.

12. Ibid., p. 40.

13. George Jacob Holyoake, *Life and Last Days of Robert Owen, of New Lanark,* p. 18.

14. George Jacob Holyoake, *Sixty Years of an Agitator's Life,* p. 115.

15. George Jacob Holyoake, *The History of Co-operation in England: Its Literature and Its Advocates,* I, p. 64.

16. Holyoake, *Sixty Years of an Agitator's Life,* p. 120.

17. Holyoake, *The History of Co-operation in England,* I, p. 80.

18. Ibid., p. 53.

19. John Brown, *Remarks on the Plans and Publication of Robert Owen, Esquire of New Lanark,* p. 28.

20. Ibid., p. 42.

21. Ibid., p. 58.

22. *The Crisis,* I, No. 9 (May 26, 1832).

23. Ibid., p. 33.

24. *Idem.*

25. Reo M. Christenson, "The Old Values Are the Best Values," in *The New York Times,* June 3, 1972, p. 29.

26. *Idem.*

27. Holyoake, *Life and Last Days of Robert Owen, of New Lanark,* pp. 16-17.

28. *Idem.*

29. Holyoake, *Robert Owen: The Precursor of Social Progress. In Justification of the Newtown Memorial,* p. 16.

31. Harriet Martineau, *Biographical Sketches,* p. 314.

APPENDIX

1. Robert Dale Owen, "An Outline of the System of Education at New Lanark" (first published 1824), pp. 81 - 103.

Selected Bibliography

PRIMARY SOURCES

1. Journals edited by Robert Owen or those expressing his views:

The Economist: a Periodical Paper explanatory of the New System of Society projected by Robert Owen, Esq., and of a Plan of Association for Improving the Condition of the Working Classes, during their Continuance at their present Employments. Jan. 27, 1821—Mar. 9, 1822.

The New Harmony Gazette. Edited by Robert Dale Owen, William Owen, and others. Oct., 1825—Oct., 1828.

The Co-operative Magazine and Monthly Herald. Jan. 1, 1826—Oct., 1828. Continued as the *London Co-operative Magazine* until 1830.

The Crisis: or, the Change from Error and Misery, to Truth and Happiness. Edited by Robert Owen and Robert Dale Owen. April, 1832—Aug., 1834.

The New Moral World: a London Weekly Publication Developing the Principles of the Rational System of Society. Edited by Robert Owen and others. Nov., 1834—Jan., 1846.

The Moral World: the Advocate of the Rational System of Society as Founded and Developed by Robert Owen. Aug., 1845—Nov., 1845.

Weekly Letters to the Human Race. Edited by Robert Owen. 1850.

Robert Owen's Journal: Explanatory of the Means to Well-Place, and Well-feed, Well-Clothe, Well-Lodge, Well-Employ, Well-Educate, Well-Govern, and Cordially Unite, the population of the world. Edited by Robert Owen. Nov., 1851—Oct., 1852.

Robert Owen's Rational Quarterly Review and Journal. Edited by Robert Owen. 1853.

Millennial Gazette: Explanatory of the Principles and Practices by which, in Peace, with Truth, Honesty, and Simplicity, the New Existence of Man upon the Earth may be easily and speedily commenced. Edited by Robert Owen. Mar., 1856—July, 1858.

2. Books

BESTOR, ARTHUR, JR. *Education and Reform at New Harmony: Correspondance of William Maclure and Marie Duclos Fretageot 1820 - 1833.* Clifton: Augustus M. Kelley, 1973 (first published 1948). Excellent introduction to the experiment at New Harmony through letters of Maclure and Fretageot.

BROWN, JOHN. *Remarks on The Plans and Publication of Robert Owen, Esquire of New Lanark.* Edinburgh: Ogle, Allardice, and Thomson, 1817. Typical criticism of Owen's theories by a minister.

DENHOLM, JAMES. *The History of the City of Glasgow & Suburbs.* Second Edition. Glasgow: R. Chapman, 1798. Brief description of New Lanark as it was under David Dale's ownership.

ENGELS, FREDERICK. *Socialism: Utopian and Scientific.* Translated by Edward Aveling. Chicago: Charles H. Kerr & Company, 1908.

FLOWER, GEORGE. *History of the English Settlement in Edwards County Illinois, Founded in 1817 and 1818, by Morris Birkbeck and George Flower.* Chicago: Fergus Printing Company, 1882. Good account of the selling of New Harmony by George Rapp to Owen.

HARRISON, JOHN F.C., ed. *Utopianism and Education: Robert Owen and the Owenites.* New York: Teachers College Press, 1968. Contains excerpts from writings by Owen and his disciples.

HAZLITT, WILLIAM. *Table Talk: Opinions on Books, Men, and Things.* Part I. New York: Wiley and Putnam, 1845. Criticism of Owen's personality and ideas by a contemporary.

HOLYOAKE, GEORGE JACOB. *The History of Co-operation in England: Its Literature and Its Advocates.* Vol. I. London: Trübner & Co., 1875. Several chapters on Owen by an admirer.

――――――――. *Sixty Years of an Agitator's Life.* Third edition, vol. I. London: T. Fisher Unwin, 1893. Anecdotal account. Describes Owen's personal appearance.

JOHNSON, OAKLEY C. *Robert Owen in the United States.* New York: Humanities Press, 1970. Reprints of important speeches given by Owen in the United States, including those delivered in Congress in 1825.

LINDLEY, HARLOW, ed. *Indiana as Seen By Early Travelers: A Collection of Reprints from Books of Travel, Letters, and Diaries Prior to 1830.* Indianapolis: Indiana Historical Commission, 1916. Excellent for firsthand accounts of life at New Harmony.

LOVETT, WILLIAM. *The Life and Struggles of William Lovett, in his Pursuit of Bread, Knowledge, and Freedom; with some short account of the different associations he belonged to, and of the opinions he entertained.* London: Trübner & Co., 1876. Mentions Owen briefly.

MACDONALD, DONALD. *The Diaries of Donald Macdonald 1824 - 1826.* Edited by Caroline Dale Snedeker. Indianapolis: Indiana Historical Society, 1942. Account of journeys to New Harmony with Robert Owen.

MARTINEAU, HARRIET. *Biographical Sketches.* London: Macmillan and Co., 1869. Personal appraisal by a woman who knew Owen.

M'Gavin, W. *The Fundamental Principles of The New Lanark System Exposed in a series of letters to Robert Owen, Esq.* Glasgow: Andrew Young, 1824. Criticism of Owen's principles.

Owen, Robert. *Book of the New Moral World.* Clifton: Augustus M. Kelley, 1970. First published in London, 1836. Owen's beliefs on the formation of character.

_____. *A Development of the Principles and Plans on which to establish Self-Supporting Home Colonies; as a Most Secure and profitable Investment for capital, and an effectual means permanently to remove the causes of ignorance, poverty, and crime; and most materially to benefit all classes of society; by giving a right application to the now greatly misdirected Powers of the Human Faculties and of Physical and Moral Science.* London: The Home Colonization Society, 1841. More of Owen's proposals.

_____. *A Discourse on A New System of Society; as delivered in the Hall of Representatives of the United States, In presence of the President of the United States, the President Elect, Heads of Departments, Members of Congress, &c. &c.* Washington: Gales & Seaton, 1825. Owen's principles.

_____. *The Life of Robert Owen,* vol. I A. New York: Augustus M. Kelley, 1967. First published 1858. Collection of documents pertaining to Owen's life and career.

_____. *The Life of Robert Owen by Himself.* New York: Alfred A. Knopf, 1920. First published 1857. Valuable source for biographical material, tempered by late age at which Owen wrote the book, relying on his memory.

_____. *A New View of Society & Other Writings.* New York: E. P. Dutton & Co., 1927. Contains essays and speeches of Owen written 1813 - 1816. Indispensable for familiarity with Owen's theories and style of writing.

_____. *The Problem of the age Solved. Manifesto of Robert Owen to the Civilized World.* Extracted from *The New York Herald,* April 14, 1847. Brief survey of Owen's accomplishments.

_____. *The Revolution in the Mind and Practice of The Human Race; or, the Coming Change from Irrationality to Rationality.* First published 1849. Clifton: Augustus M. Kelley, 1973.

Owen, Robert Dale. "An Outline of the System of Education at New Lanark," in *Robert Owen at New Lanark: Two Booklets and One Pamphlet 1824 - 1838.* Advisory ed., Kenneth E. Carpenter. New York: Arno Press, 1972. An indispensable aid to understanding Owen's system of education.

_____. *Threading My Way.* London: Trübner & Co., 1874. Account of life as a youth in the Owen family by Owen's most famous son.

OWEN, WILLIAM. *Diary of William Owen November 1824 — April 1825.* Edited by Joel W. Hiatt. Indianapolis: The Bobbs-Merrill Company, 1906. Detailed account by Owen's son.

PEARS, THOMAS and SARAH. *New Harmony: An Adventure in Happiness — The Papers of Thomas and Sarah Pears.* Edited by Thomas Clinton Pears, Jr. Indianapolis: Indiana Historical Society, 1933. Excellent account of the disappointments and hardships many experienced at New Harmony.

SILVER, HAROLD, ed. *Robert Owen on Education.* Cambridge, England: University Press, 1969. Contains samplings from Owen's writings and speeches pertaining to his theories of education. Good way to get acquainted with Owen's works.

TROLLOPE, MRS. FRANCES. *Domestic Manners of the Americans.* New York: Dodd, Mead & Company, 1901. First published 1832. Brief description of Owen's speaking manner by an observer.

3. Parliamentary Documents

British Sessional Papers, 1816, vol. IV. Edited by Edgar L. Erickson.
_____, 1820, vol. XII. Edited by Edgar L. Erickson.

4. Pamphlets

HOLYOAKE, GEORGE JACOB. *Life and Last Days of Robert Owen, of New Lanark.* Centenary Edition. London: Trübner & Co., 1871. Owen's final illness and burial. In praise of Owen's theories.

_____. *Robert Owen: The Precursor of Social Progress. In Justification of the Newtown Memorial.* Manchester: The Co-operative Union Limited, 1900. Very brief summary of Owen's accomplishments.

M'KNIGHT, JAMES, *A Discourse Exposing Robert Owen's System, as Practised by the Franklin Community at Haverstraw.* New York: John Gray & Co., 1826. M'Knight, a member of the Franklin community, expresses disillusionment with Owen's theories, particularly those pertaining to religion.

Mr. Owen's proposed Arrangements for The Distressed Working Classes, shown to be consistent with Sound Principles of Political Economy: in Three Letters addressed to David Ricardo, Esq. M.P. London: Longman, Hurst, Rees. Orme, and Brown, 1819. Probably written by Robert Owen. Describes development of New Lanark under Owen's direction, and economic plans for improving the condition of the poor.

SECONDARY SOURCES

1. Books

ARNDT, KARL J. R. *George Rapp's Harmony Society 1785 - 1847.* Cranbury: Associated University Presses, Inc., 1972 edition. First published

1965. Interesting background information on the Rappites in Württemberg, in Pennsylvania, and in Indiana.

BARNARD, H. C. *A History of English Education From 1760.* London: University of London Press, 1969. Good background on educational system in Owen's time.

BEER, MAX. *A History of British Socialism.* London: George Allen and Unwin Ltd., 1940. (First published 1919). Sets Owenite socialism in the context of other such movements.

BESTOR, ARTHUR. *Backwoods Utopias: The Sectarian and Owenite Phases of Communitarian Socialism in America: 1663 - 1829.* Philadelphia: University of Pennsylvania Press, 1967. First published 1950. Excellent comparative study of New Harmony and other Owenite communities; good information on Owen's reception in the United States.

BUTT, JOHN, ed. *Robert Owen: Aspects of his Life and Work.* New York: Humanities Press, 1971. Essays on various aspects of Owen's theories. Note especially Margery Browning, "Owen as an Educator," pp. 52-75.

COLE, G.D.H. *Robert Owen.* Boston: Little, Brown, and Company, 1925. Good biography of Owen and his times.

COLE, MARGARET. *Robert Owen of New Lanark.* New York: Oxford University Press, 1953. Outline of Owen's life and career. Information taken from Owen's autobiography.

CURTIS, S. J. *History of Education in Great Britain.* Westport: Greenwood Press, 1971. Third edition. First published 1948. Very detailed account of education in Britain.

A Cyclopedia of Education. Edited by Paul Monroe. New York: The Macmillan Company, 1911. Brief accounts of nineteenth century educators.

DEWEY, JOHN. *Democracy and Education.* New York: The Macmillan Company, 1916. A significant introduction to Dewey's philosophy of education.

DICKENS, CHARLES. *The Life & Adventures of Nicholas Nickleby.* London: Oxford University Press, 1957. Famous novel written in 1838 - 1839, dramatizing conditions of the poor in England.

Dictionary of National Biography. Edited by Leslie Stephens. New York: Macmillan and Company, 1885. Good thumbnail sketches of important British persons.

GARNETT, R. G. *Co-operation and the Owenite socialist communities in Britain, 1825 - 45.* Manchester: Manchester University Press, 1972. Owen's influence, as seen in the communities organized by his followers.

GOSDEN, P.H.J.H. *How They Were Taught: An Anthology of Contem-*

porary Accounts of Learning and Teaching in England 1800 - 1950.
Oxford: Basil Blackwell, 1969. Interesting contemporary accounts of
education system in Great Britain.

HARRISON, J. F. C. *Robert Owen and the Owenites in Britain and America:
The* Quest *for the New Moral World.* London: Routledge and Kegan
Paul, 1969. Concentrates on socialist theories of Owen. Contains
good chapter on Owenite communities and excellent bibliography.

HARVEY, ROWLAND HILL. *Robert Owen Social Idealist.* Berkeley: University
of California Press, 1949. Good background on the Industrial Revolution. Deals at length with problems at New Harmony.

LEOPOLD, RICHARD WILLIAM. *Robert Dale Owen: A Biography.* Cambridge:
Harvard University Press, 1940. Contains some details of Robert Dale
Owen's childhood, as well as information on the adult lives of Owen's
children.

LOCKWOOD, GEORGE B. *The New Harmony Movement.* New York: D.
Appleton and Company, 1905. Excellent book. Compares Owen's
communities with other systems.

MIDWINTER, ERIC. *Nineteenth Century Education.* London: Longman
Group Limited, 1970. Good background.

PODMORE, FRANK. *Robert Owen: A Biography.* New York: D. Appleton and
Company, 1924. Excellent detailed account of Owen's life and works.

POLLARD, SIDNEY and JOHN SALT, eds. *Robert Owen Prophet of the Poor:
Essays in Honour of the Two Hundredth Anniversary of his Birth.*
Lewisburg: Bucknell University Press, 1971. Essays assessing Owen's
reputation as businessman, educator, and father of English socialism.

RUSK, ROBERT R. *A History of Infant Education.* London: University of
London Press, Ltd., 1933. Theories of educators.

SNEDEKER, CAROLINE DALE. *The Town of the Fearless.* Garden City:
Doubleday, Doran & Company, Inc., 1931. Background information
on people active at New Harmony.

TAWNEY, R. H. *The Radical Tradition: Twelve Essays on Politics, Education, and Literature.* Edited by Rita Hinden. London: George Allen
& Unwin Ltd., 1964. Contains one chapter on Owen which focuses
primarily on labor and the cooperative movement.

THOMPSON, E. P. *The Making of the English Working Class.* New York:
Vintage Books, 1963. To understand the change brought on by the
Industrial Revolution, no book is more useful. Chapter on Owenism
deals with Owen's effect on the working class.

TREVELYAN, GEORGE MACAULAY. *British History in the Nineteenth Century
and After (1782 - 1919).* London: Longmans, Green and Co., 1937.
Interesting part on Owen's influence.

TYLER, ALICE FELT. *Freedom's Ferment: Phases of American Social History from the Colonial Period to the Outbreak of the Civil War.* New York: Harper and Row, 1962. First published 1944. Owenism presented as one form of American social experimentation, growing out of American religious traditions, Jeffersonianism, and frontier democracy.

WALLAS, GRAHAM. *The Life of Francis Place 1771 - 1854.* London: Longmans, Green, and Co., 1898. Quotes Place on Owen.

WILSON, WILLIAM E. *The Angel and the Serpent: The Story of New Harmony.* Bloomington: Indiana University Press, 1964. The Rappites and the Owenites at New Harmony.

2. Articles

ESTABROOK, ARTHUR H. "The Family History of Robert Owen." *Indiana Magazine of History* XIX, No. 1 (Mar. 1923), pp. 63-101. Good information about Owen's descendants.

3. Bibliographies

NATIONAL LIBRARY OF WALES. *A Bibliography of Robert Owen, the Socialist, 1771 - 1858.* Aberystwyth, 1914/2nd edition 1925.

SHIGERU, GOTO. *Robert Owen 1771 - 1858: a New Bibliographical Study.* 2 vols. Osaka, Japan, 1932 - 34. In Japanese and English.

UNIVERSITY OF LONDON. *Robert Owen, 1771 - 1858. Catalogue of an Exhibition of Printed Books Held in the Library of the University of London, October—December 1858.* London, 1959.

Index